BREAKING THE

VAMPIRE'S

CURSE

THE MISSING PIECE

IN MANIFESTING

WEALTH

BREAKING THE VAMPIRE'S CURSE

THE MISSING PIECE IN MANIFESTING WEALTH

BY

AMY LAW

Published by Kududa

ISBN: 979-8-9914171-1-2

TABLE OF CONTENTS

INTRODUCTION

Welcome to Breaking the Vampire's Curse: The Missing Piece in Manifesting Wealth. This book presents a new way of approaching the process of understanding, healing, and growth for individuals who have lived through toxic family dynamics. It provides practical tools to reclaim power, manifest dreams, and achieve financial success despite toxic influences, instilling a sense of empowerment and hope in its readers.

The narrative of this book is a compelling story of overcoming bullying within family and extended family dynamics, ultimately leading to extraordinary success. It explores the devastating effects of covert bullying and illustrates how breaking free from toxic environments leads to unimaginable prosperity. With valuable insights into the complex connections between trauma, resilience, and growth, the book offers a comprehensive perspective on healing and empowerment.

True wealth comes from understanding the energy that shapes one's life and fully tapping into inherent potential. People often recognize bullying in its overt forms, like physical aggression or name-calling, but they may overlook a more subtle and insidious form: covert bullying. Covert bullying uses emotional manipulation and psychological tactics to erode confidence and self-worth. It leaves no visible scars, but its effects are profound, especially within family dynamics. Using the metaphor of 'Breaking the Vampire's Curse,' this book illustrates how covert bullies, like vampires, drain their targets of energy, confidence, and potential. It offers strategies and insights for breaking free from this curse, re-claiming power, and thriving in all aspects of life.

Achieving success in the face of toxic family dynamics is not just desirable; it's essential and empowering. This transformation requires shifting mindsets, embracing growth, and overcoming psychological challenges. It is a solo journey of self-discovery, relying on inner strength and resilience. Through practical advice, personal stories, and powerful metaphors, this book guides readers in navigating toxic relationships, overcoming covert bullying, and manifesting wealth. It views challenges as opportunities for growth, emphasizing the importance of solitude and forgiveness. These elements bring peace and reassurance, guiding you on the steps needed to succeed.

This book's comprehensive approach makes it distinct, drawing from cultural, religious, and historical perspectives to offer a deeper understanding of healing and success. It provides concrete steps to help individuals heal from covert bullying and achieve financial and emotional success, addressing the emotional, psychological, and practical aspects of overcoming bullying. As the journey of self-discovery unfolds, it is essential to recognize that many others have faced similar struggles with covert bullying and have emerged stronger, more resilient, and victorious in their pursuit of success. This book demonstrates how to turn challenges into strength, fostering personal and financial growth.

Breaking the Vampire's Curse offers more than just guidance; it is a comprehensive roadmap to unlocking full potential and living a life of abundance and fulfillment. It serves as a beacon of hope, proving that transformation is within reach for anyone ready to break free from limitations and claim the life they deserve. This comprehensive roadmap guides and supports your journey to success, providing a sense of reassurance and direction.

THE HIDDEN VEIL OF COVERT BULLYING

In the silent depths of our homes and the hidden recesses of our hearts, the ominous specter of covert bullying often casts its shadow, entwining itself with the very fabric of our existence. It's a story that profoundly connects with many—a journey marked by pain, isolation, shame, and the overwhelming burden of self-doubt and self-loathing. It's a relentless quest for validation amidst a landscape of unrelenting cruelty. Here, within the veiled confines of our most intimate connections, a subtle yet venomous form of bullying finds fertile ground to take root and flourish. This covert battleground is the breeding ground for the most insidious manipulation, control, and betrayal strategies. Though unseen, the wounds it inflicts cut deep into the very core of one's being, leaving scars that endure long after the physical bruises have healed.

Within the realm of familial and relational dynamics, the scars of psychological warfare bear witness to the enduring legacy of vampirism hosting—a legacy that defies the passage of time, persisting in the echoes of whispered taunts and veiled threats. For too long, the scourge of hosting has been confined to the realms of playgrounds and schoolyards, dismissed as a mere rite of passage on the journey to adulthood. Yet, the reality is far more nuanced and sinister. Covert bullying, a universal experience that transcends age, gender, and race, infiltrates even the most cherished bonds—our families. At the core of our exploration is the crucial realization that covert bullying is not an isolated incident but a deeply ingrained behavior—a lasting manifestation of power struggles, manipulation, and control.

As we embark on this journey of self-reflection, we navigate the complex terrain of familial dysfunction, unraveling the intricate fabric of social dynamics and cultural norms that perpetuate the cycle of abuse. It's a path that demands courage, empathy, and a resolute determination to confront the hidden darkness within. By shining a light on the concealed aspects of covert bullying, our aim is to empower individuals to reclaim their voices, dignity, and self-worth. Through understanding and awareness, we strive to dismantle the structures of oppression and foster a future where every individual is valued, respected, and supported on their path to healing and liberation.

Let's embark on a journey to unravel the insidious veil of covert bullying, tracing its origins back to childhood. We will explore the complex web of familial dynamics and societal norms perpetuating its existence. In the chapters of this book, we will thoroughly examine the essence of covert bullying, delving into all its facets and uncovering its roots in childhood.

CHILDHOOD SHADOWS

Childhood is a time of innocence, characterized by carefree play and boundless imagination. However, for many children, this idealized image of childhood is shattered by the harsh reality of familial discord and emotional manipulation. Childhood bullying within the family is a profoundly troubling phenomenon with lifelong repercussions for the target and their loved ones.

The wounds etched onto the emotional body during these formative years may never fully heal. Consider the plight of a child trapped in the tumult of family strife—a vulnerable target for ridicule, scorn, and manipulation at the hands of those closest to them. This scenario plays out frequently, leaving indelible scars on the target's psyche and soul, wounds that may take a lifetime to heal and they can never heal without soul-searching.

Children are like clean canvases of pure energy; when that energy is tainted, the consequences are significant. This pure energy is essential for achieving their potential in adulthood; therefore, anyone who affects a child's energy through covert bullying essentially undermines that child's prospects.

Within the family unit, where love and support are expected to flourish, covert Bullying can take root and thrive. Whether perpetrated by parents, siblings, or other relatives, emotional manipulation and psychological warfare inflicted upon a child or young adult can have profound and lasting effects, shaping their self-image, self-respect, self-value, relationships, and worldview for years to come. One of the most profound and heartbreaking consequences of childhood bullying within the family dynamic is the erosion of the target's sense of self-worth and identity.

Children naturally look to their family members as sources of love, support, and validation, forming the bedrock of their developing psyche. However, when they are met with ridicule, scorn, or emotional manipulation instead of nurturing care, their fragile sense of self can be shattered beyond repair. This betrayal of trust leaves them feeling deeply unworthy, unloved, and utterly isolated, as the very individuals meant to protect and cherish them become perpetrators of emotional harm. What makes this form of Bullying especially insidious is its covert nature, often occurring behind the parents' backs and unseen by others.

Covert Bullying leaves the child incredibly lonely, as no one else can see the abuse but the child, and it continues to erode the child's self-esteem without detection. Adults, relatives, or other siblings who bully a younger sibling always operate in the shadows, exploiting the innocence and vulnerability of childhood to perpetuate their harmful behavior without facing the consequences. This covert approach amplifies the damage inflicted on the target, as they are left to grapple with the pain and confusion alone, unable to seek help or support.

Bullying done in the dark has the most severe impact precisely because it goes unnoticed and unaddressed. Without the intervention of parents or other authority figures, the target is left defenseless against the relentless onslaught of emotional abuse. Their suffering is compounded by feelings of shame and isolation, further isolating them from sources of comfort and protection.

Imagine a child constantly belittled by a parent, older sibling, or relative. They are subjected to cruel taunts and disparaging remarks that chip away at their self-esteem and confidence. Each insult serves as a dagger to the heart, leaving wounds that may never fully heal. Over time, the child internalizes these negative messages believing they are inherently flawed or unworthy of love and acceptance.

Moreover, the emotional scars inflicted by childhood bullying can extend far beyond the home, permeating every aspect of the target's life. They may struggle to form healthy relationships with peers at school, fearing rejection or judgment at every turn. In social settings, they may feel like outsiders, unable to shake the lingering shame and inadequacy instilled by their family members. Even in adulthood, these wounds can persist, leading to low self-worth, depression, anxiety, or other mental health challenges that impede one's ability to live a fulfilling life.

The cycle of abuse and manipulation perpetuated within the family can reverberate through future generations, creating a legacy of pain and dysfunction passed down from parent to child. When Bullying causes psychological distress that compromises a child's health, its effects ripple through the child's life and profoundly affect the parents who witness their suffering. This is especially evident as the long-term effects of bullying become more apparent later in life.

The anguish of witnessing their beloved child endure such pain adds to a layer of emotional burden on the family, contributing to a cycle of distress and dysfunction. Consequently, the comparison to Bullying conducted in secrecy underscores the profound and enduring consequences of this hidden form of abuse. It can deeply scar the target's psyche and soul, reverberating throughout the entire family for years to come.

As a society, we must recognize the pervasive nature of familial Covert Bullying and work tirelessly to create safe, nurturing, respectful environments where children can thrive and grow without fear of emotional harm. Only by doing so can we break the cycle of abuse and pave the way for a brighter future for generations to come. This is a responsibility we all share, and it's one that we must take seriously. Acknowledging the pain and trauma inflicted by inconspicuous Bullying is the first step toward healing. We delve into the emotional landscape of anger, grief, and betrayal, offering practical guidance on navigating the path to forgiveness and liberation.

Through stories of resilience, courage, and empowerment, we offer hope to those who feel trapped in the grip of childhood abuse, showing that, even though the pain may persist long after leaving the household, it is still possible to overcome it.

Healing and transformation are possible, even in the darkest of times. The target is all alone in this, and the repercussions can lead to the downfall of their lives and broken dreams if they don't understand the magnitude of the abuse they have endured. The effects extend beyond the immediate family, rippling into every aspect of their existence. Friends become adversaries, allies turn away, and the very foundation of their social fabric begins to fray under the weight of cruelty.

In conclusion, covert Bullying within families and among relatives is a pervasive yet often overlooked issue with devastating consequences for targets. Tactics such as gaslighting, scapegoating, passive-aggressive behavior and relational aggression are varied and insidious, leaving deep emotional scars.

ORIGIN AND EVOLUTION OF VAMPIRES

The idea of vampires, born from early human attempts to explain natural phenomena, death, and disease, has a captivating and enduring power.

Ancient civilizations crafted stories about demonic beings, such as Lilitu in Mesopotamian mythology and Lamia in Greek mythology, who preyed on the living. These early myths laid the foundation for the vampire legends that continue to evolve and persist in different forms today, captivating and intriguing us with their enduring power.

Fear of Death, Disease & Misunderstanding of Bodies

Throughout history, death and illness have been sources of mystery and fear. When loved ones fell ill or died suddenly, people often turned to supernatural explanations. Diseases like tuberculosis and plagues were sometimes attributed to vampires, believed to feed on the life force of living. The natural process of decomposition also fueled these beliefs—people interpreted signs like blood seeping from the mouth or hair and nails appearing to grow after death as evidence that the dead were still alive and feeding on others.

Historical Context and Folklore

The belief in vampires has deep roots across various cultures,

 with many unique elements contributing to the myth. While scientific evidence for the existence of supernatural vampires is lacking, the symbolic power of these myths has endured. Superstition and Vampire Hunts During the Middle Ages, people often attributed unexplained deaths and illnesses to vampires. Communities exhumed bodies and staked them through the heart to stop the dead from rising. These rituals reflected fear, superstition, and a misunderstanding of death and disease.

Scientific Explanations for Vampiric Traits

The vampire myth, a tale that has haunted cultures for centuries, is now being recontextualized in the light of historical and scientific understanding. Many researchers believe this myth originates in scientific and medical phenomena that were misunderstood in earlier times, particularly during periods of limited medical knowledge and widespread fear of the unknown. These conditions and natural processes once misinterpreted as signs of vampirism, have now been explained by science, offering a new perspective on the legends we know today.

Decomposition: During a body's natural de composition, certain traits that resemble those of vampires may appear. As the body breaks down, blood and other fluids can ooze from the mouth, which might have been interpreted as evidence of a corpse drinking blood. Additionally, the skin retracts as

it decomposes, making it look like hair and nails are still growing, further fueling beliefs that the dead were still "alive" in some form

Porphyria: Porphyria, a rare genetic disorder, has been suggested to explain vampire legends. This condition makes the skin extremely sensitive to sunlight, as vampires are said to

avoid the sun. Severe cases of porphyria can also cause disfigurement and gum recession, making the teeth appear more prominent, which could have contributed to image of the fanged vampires.

Rabies: Rabies outbreaks in history may have played a sig-

nificant role in shaping vampire myths due to several critical symptoms of the disease that resemble traditional vampire traits:

Sensitivity to Light: People infected with rabies can develop extreme sensitivity to light, similar to how vampires are often depicted as avoiding sunlight.

Aggression and Madness: Rabies affects the central nervous system, leading to aggressive behavior, confusion, and a propensity for violence, all traits associated with vampires.

Biting: Rabies can cause people and animals to become hyper-aggressive, sometimes leading to biting, which parallels the vampire's need to bite and draw blood from targets.

Fear of Water (Hydrophobia): One of the more unusual symptoms of rabies is hydrophobia or fear of water. In some vampire's legends. Vampires are said to avoid running water, a potential link to this symptom.

Transmission through Bites: Similar to rabies, vampirism in folklore is frequently portrayed as being transmitted through bites.

The concept of being "transformed" into a vampire after being bitten parallels the way rabies spreads through the bite of an infected individual or animal.

Blood Disorders:

Some blood disorders, including anemia and iron deficiencies, may have contributed to the vampire myth. People suffering from these conditions often have pale skin and can experience

fatigue and weakness, which may have led to beliefs about the need to "consume" blood for strength and vitality.

These scientific phenomena offer plausible explanations for many traits historically attributed to vampires. In times when medical knowledge was limited, these misunderstood conditions likely fueled the fear of the supernatural, leading to the creation of the vampire myth leading to the creation of the vampire myth to explain unusual and frightening behaviors.

Modern-Day Vampires in Metaphors and Subcultures

In contemporary culture, three main types of modern-day "vampires" are often discussed metaphorically or in subcultures: Sanguinarians, Psychic Vampires, and Emotional Vampires:

Sanguinarians:

These individuals believe they must consume human or animal blood to maintain their physical, emotional, or spiritual well-being. Their practice of blood consumption is consensual,

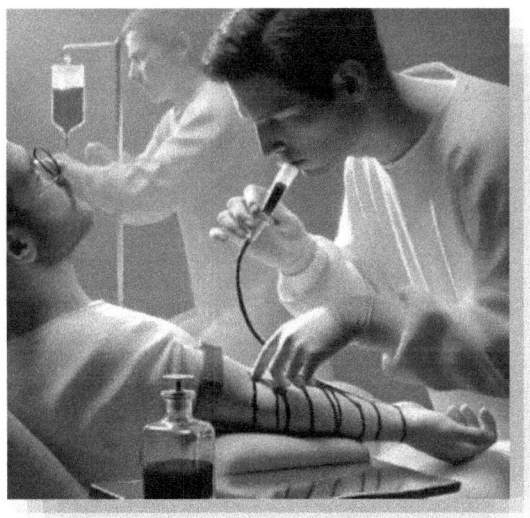

typically involving safety precautions. However, the psychological impact on donors remains an area that warrants greater empathy and consideration.

Psychic Vampires:or Energy vampires, do not consume blood but instead drain the life force or energy from others, leaving them emotionally exhausted. It might be unintentional, but the presence of such individuals can disrupt the psychic balance of those around them.

Emotional Vampires: often described in psychological terms, drain the emotional energy of those around them through manipulative behaviors such as excessive neediness, negativity,

guilt-tripping, or targetization. They deplete others emotionally, leading to frustration and exhaustion.

Cultural Influence of Vampires in Literature
&
Media

Literature and Film: Vampire stories have captivated audiences for centuries. Works like Bram Stoker's *Dracula* and modern franchises such as *Twilight* and *True Blood* keep the vampire myth alive in popular culture. These stories explore themes of immortality, fear, desire, and the darker impulses of human nature.

Goth and Vampire Subcultures: Subcultures that value mystery, allure, and fascination with the supernatural embrace vampire aesthetics and mythology. These movements embed the concept of vampirism into contemporary fashion, charm, and lifestyle.

Ancient Origins of the Vampire Myth

The concept of vampires' dates back to ancient civilizations, where various myths and legends shaped the vampire lore we recognize today.

Ancient Mesopotamia and Greece

In Greek mythology, creatures like **Lamia** and **Empusa** preyed on young men and children, drinking their blood. In Mesopotamian myths, figures like **Lilitu** and **Lamashtu** drank the blood of infants and preg-

nant women, embodying primal fears of death and danger.

Chinese Jiangshi A reanimated corpse that feeds on the life force (Qi) of the living. These "hopping vampires" represent fear of death returning to haunt the living.

Indian Vetala:
A spirit that possesses corpses and drains life energy from the living. The Vetala preys on humans by inhabiting the dead mirroring the themes of control and hostility in other vampire myths.

Romanian folklore includes undead spirits like **Strigoi** and

Moroi, who rise from the grave to drink the blood of the living.

Slavic legends of **Upir** and **Nosferatu** laid the groundwork for many modern vampire traits.

Vlad the Impaler

Ruler of 15th-century Wallachia, Vlad III was infamous for im-

paling enemies. His surname "Dracula" and his association with blood and violence inspired Bram Stoker's *Dracula*, creating one of the most iconic vampire figures in literature.

Early Modern period
Countess Elizabeth Báthory

People accused Báthory of torturing and killing young women, with rumors claiming she bathed in their blood to preserve her youth, which further embedded the connection between blood, beauty, and vampiric immortality.

Modern Era

The Vampyre:*18th and 19th Century Literature:*

John Polidori's 1819 novella introduced the aristocratic vampire.

Varney the Vampire

A mid-19th-century serial novel introduces a sympathetic vampire struggling with his monstrous nature

Bram Stoker's Dracula: In 1897, this novel solidified many characteristics that define modern vampires, such as immortality, aversion to sunlight, and the need for human blood.

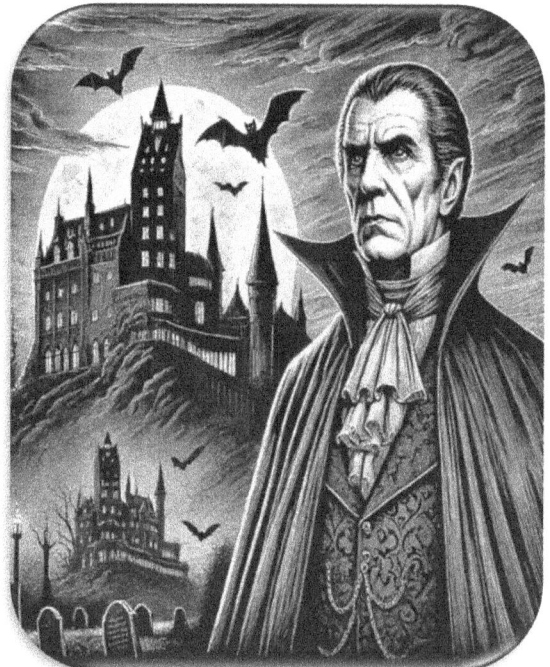

MODERN VAMPIRISM

BLENDING TRADITION WITH CONTEMPORARY THEMES

Modern vampire narratives have evolved to reinterpret traditional vampire lore, adding innovative twists that reflect contemporary issues. These stories preserve the allure of classic myths while exploring new dimensions of character and society. This evolution keeps the genre fresh and intriguing, appealing to readers who are interested in the progression of literary themes.

Complex Character Dynamics: In modern narratives, vampires are no longer just bloodthirsty villains. They are depicted as emotionally complex beings who wrestle with internal conflicts such as immortality, loneliness, guilt, and the search for meaning. By humanizing vampires, these stories make their struggles more relatable, allowing audiences to connect with their emotional journeys.

Symbolism and Metaphors: Vampires often serve as metaphors for real-world struggles, such as addiction, fear of the unknown, and moral dilemmas. These narratives delve into darker human impulses, using vampirism as a lens to explore the psychological and ethical challenges people face. This symbolic approach adds layers of depth to the vampire myth.

Reimagining Classic Tropes: While modern vampire stories respect traditional weaknesses—like vulnerability to sunlight— they often reinterpret these elements to fit into contemporary society. For example, some vampires may use protective clothing or medical advancements to survive in the daylight. These creative solutions keep the genre fresh and relevant.

Technological Integration: In today's world, vampires adapt to technology like humans. They use social media to maintain anonymity, employ surveillance to stay ahead of threats, and even rely on medical advancements to preserve their immortality. This technology integration makes modern vampires more relatable and grounded in the present day.

Diversity and Inclusion: Recent vampire stories increasingly reflect the diversity of today's society. Characters come from various cultural backgrounds, genders, and sexual orientations, breaking away from traditional stereotypes and making the genre more inclusive. This shift adds complexity and richness to vampire narratives, aligning them with contemporary values.From their ancient origins in Mesopotamian and Greek myths to their modern adaptations in literature, film, and popular culture, vampires have remained one of the most enduring figures in the human imagination. By blending traditional elements with contemporary themes—such as emotional complexity, symbolism, technology, and diversity, vampire myths continue to captivate audiences across cultures and generations.

From their ancient origins in Mesopotamian and Greek myths to their modern adaptations in literature, film, and popular culture, vampires have remained one of the most enduring figures in the human imagination. By blending traditional elements with contemporary themes—such as emotional complexity, symbolism, technology, and diversity—vampire myths continue to captivate audiences across cultures and generations.

THE INSIGHTFUL METAPHOR OF ENERGY VAMPIRES

The metaphor of energy vampires' sheds light on the complexities of human behavior, especially within families, where power, control, and manipulation can profoundly impact relationships. By comparing vampire mythology and covert bullying, we better understand how individuals within families may exploit others for their own benefit.

This metaphor helps reveal the hidden dynamics of manipulation. It encourages us to challenge ourselves and break free from these influences, stressing the urgent need to foster a more compassionate and equitable family environment where every member feels valued and supported.

Understanding these dynamics becomes crucial as we navigate human interactions, especially within families. This section serves as a guide to overcoming the shadows cast by covert bullying, revealing its hidden mechanisms. Through this metaphor, readers are equipped with the tools to recognize manipulation and reclaim their emotional autonomy, fostering healthier relationships.

The vampire analogy empowers targets and their families to break free from toxic dynamics while fostering a sense of connection and engagement in readers.

Vampires as a Metaphor for Covert Bullying

For instance, a parent who constantly undermines their child's self-esteem or a sibling who manipulates others to get their way can be seen as engaging in 'emotional vampirism. These individuals can be seen as inflicting deep psychological damage, preying on their targets in a way that leaves them emotionally drained. Like mythical vampires, covert bullies break the spirit of their targets, leaving behind emotional and psychological scars that can persist across generations.

Inherent Nature of Covert Bullies

Covert bullies, like their mythical vampire counterparts, often seem to possess an inherent nature. Their tendencies toward manipulation and control usually appear innate rather than resulting from external influences. On the surface, they may appear perfectly normal, fulfilling their family roles and maintaining outward appearances. Yet beneath this facade, they subtly drain their targets of happiness, success, and emotional well-being.

Psychological Impact of Covert Bullying

The emotional toll of covert bullying is profound. Targets often experience deep psychological damage, leaving them emotionally depleted and struggling with long-lasting effects. Much like vampires draining the life force from their targets, covert bullies leave behind emotional exhaustion and trauma that can resonate across generations.

Recognizing the psychological impact of this abuse is crucial as it fosters empathy and helps bring awareness to the lasting harm caused by covert bullying, making the audience feel more empathetic and understanding.

COMPARING VAMPIRISM AND COVERT

BULLYING

The parallels between vampirism and covert bullying are striking. Both operate through deception and manipulation, draining the energy of their targets. The impact of this emotional and psychological exploitation leaves lasting scars. By examining these shared traits, we gain a deeper understanding of how both phenomena function—vampirism symbolizing the predatory nature of covert bullies who exploit the vulnerability of their targets for personal gain.

This metaphor encourages us to recognize, understand, and combat the insidious effects of covert bullying. By shedding light on these dark aspects of human behavior, we can work towards healing, resilience, and transformation, ensuring families become safe spaces free from manipulation. Setting boundaries, seeking support, and practicing self-care can help combat covert bullying. The vampire metaphor deepens our understanding and empowers us to create a more compassionate and emotionally healthy society.

Selection and Targets

Vampires

Selection Criteria: Vampires select their targets based on opportunity, vulnerability, and the potential to sustain their existence. They prefer individuals who are isolated, emotionally fragile, or susceptible to their allure and manipulation.

Types of Targets:

The Lonely and Isolated: Individuals who are alone or lack a support network are prime targets, as their isolation makes them easier to control.

The Emotionally Vulnerable: Those experiencing emotional turmoil or significant life changes are more susceptible to a vampire's charm and influence.

The Naive and Trusting: Those who are overly trusting or naive may more easily fall prey to a vampire's deceptive tactics.

The Unaware and Unprotected: Due to their lack of preparedness, individuals unaware of or who do not believe in vampires are easier targets.

The Youthful and Innocent: Young and innocent individuals are often targeted for their purity and life force, making them appealing to vampires.

Covert Bullies

Selection Criteria:

Covert bullies choose their targets based on vulnerability and opportunity. They seek out individuals less likely to retaliate or in

positions where the bully's actions can go unnoticed.

Types of Targets:

The Socially Isolated: Like vampires, covert bullies often target individuals who lack support networks, making them more vulnerable to manipulation and control.

The Emotionally Fragile: Those undergoing emotional stress are prime targets for covert bullies.

The Perceived Weak: Individuals perceived as weak, either due to personality, social status, or other factors, are frequently targeted.

The Non-Confrontational: Covert bullies often choose the non-confrontational as easy targets. They avoid conflict and are less likely to stand up for them-selves.

The Potential: Familial covert bul-lies target individuals with potential out of jealousy, aiming to under-mine their success and confidence.

Method of Energy Drain

Vampires: Vampires use their supernatural abilities to seduce, hypnotize and ultimately feed on their targets' blood. This act is a metaphor for the draining of life force and vitality, leaving the target weakened and dependent on the vampire.

Covert Bullies

Covert bullies use psychological tactics to undermine and control their targets, including:

Gaslighting: Making the target doubt their perceptions and reality.

Spreading Rumors: Damaging the target's reputation and social standing and relationships through subtle and insidious rumors.

Exclusion and Isolation: Purposefully excluding the target from social or professional circles.

Passive-Aggressive Behavior: Using indirect aggression to belittle or undermine the target.

Undermining Confidence: Constantly criticizing or questioning the target's abilities and decisions.

The Vampire's Neck Bite

Vampires

Marks of Vulnerability: Vampires leave bite marks on the neck as evidence of feeding. These marks serve as a signal to other vampires that the person has been a target before. That makes them a likely target for future attacks, as the target is now marked as vulnerable and more accessible to prey upon.

Covert Bullies

Marks of Vulnerability: Similarly, the psychological scars left by covert bullying can make an individual more susceptible to further manipulation. The emotional damage and eroded self-esteem serve as invisible "marks" that other bullies can detect. And that often leads to a pattern where the target continues to encounter covert bullying throughout their life.

Long-Term Vulnerability

Vampires

Once a vampire bites someone, other vampires may find the target more attractive because of their weakened state and the visible bite marks. This continuous state of vulnerability means they must remain vigilant and find ways to protect themselves from further attacks.

Covert Bullies

Targets of covert bullying often find themselves repeatedly targeted in different environments, such as new workplaces, social circles, or even within their own families. The initial trauma and diminished self-worth can make them appear as easier targets, perpetuating a cycle of targetization.

Impact on Targets

Vampires: The mark left by a vampire can lead to physical and emotional depletion, making the target weaker and more dependent on their predator. The visible mark serves as a reminder of their encounter and a warning to others of their vulnerability.

Covert Bullies: The psychological and emotional impact of covert bullying leads to long-term mental health challenges. Targets often struggle with anxiety, depression, and a lack of self-esteem. These effects can make it difficult for them to form healthy relationships and succeed in various aspects of life, perpetuating their vulnerability to further bullying.

Psychological Domination

Vampires: Vampires often use mind control, creating a sense of helplessness and dependency.

Covert Bullies: Covert bullies dominate their targets psychologically by eroding their self-esteem and creating dependency through manipulation. That highlights the need for self-awareness and empowerment in dealing with such situations.

Charismatic Facade

Vampires: Vampires typically possess a magnetic personality, drawing people to them and masking their true nature

Covert Bullies: Covert bullies often possess a strong sense of charisma. They use their charm to manipulate social dynamics and sway others against their targets while maintaining control and influence.

Fear and Intimidation

Vampires: Vampires instill fear in their targets using their supernatural powers and the threat of violence.

Covert Bullies: Covert bullies instill fear through subtle threats, social exclusion, and undermining their target's self-worth.

Exploitation of Trust

Vampires: Vampires exploit their targets' trust by presenting themselves as protectors or allies, only to reveal their predatory nature when the target is most vulnerable.

Covert Bullies: Covert bullies position themselves as friends or confidants, using the target's trust to gather information and exploit their vulnerabilities. Until they have fully drained their life force. Covert bullies can be equally relentless, persistently targeting the same individual over an extended period, gradually eroding their targets' resilience and breaking down their self-image, effectively dismantling their protective defenses.

Adaptability and Persistence

Vampires: Vampires adapt to different cultures and times, changing their methods to suit environments and maintain relevance.

Covert Bullies: Covert bullies adjust their tactics to various situations, whether in families, workplaces, or social groups, ensuring their methods remain effective.

Social and Cultural Universality

Vampires: Vampires appear in myths and stories across all races, cultures, and religions, symbolizing universal fears and desires.

Covert Bullies: Covert bullying is a universal phenomenon that transcends racial, cultural, and religious boundaries, manifesting in different forms but always with the same underlying dynamics.

Secrecy and Stealth

Vampires: Vampires operate in the shadows, using secrecy and stealth to avoid detection and continue predatory ways.

Covert Bullies: Covert bullies also operate in secrecy, using subtle and insidious methods to avoid being caught or exposed.

BATTLING COVERT BULLIES
METAPHORICAL COMPARISON VANQUISHING VAMPIRES

Exposure to Truth

Vampires: Sunlight weakens or destroys vampires.

Covert Bullies: Exposing the truth can weaken the covert bully's power by bringing covert bullying behaviors to light. Transparency and openness act like sunlight, revealing the bully's actions and preventing them from operating in the shadows. For instance, sharing documented evidence of the bully's actions with trusted individuals or authorities can help expose and address the behavior.

Setting Boundaries

Vampires: Garlic wards off vampires, keeping them at a safe distance.

Covert Bullies: Establishing and enforcing clear boundaries deters covert bullies. Consistent personal and professional boundaries act like garlic, creating a barrier that bullies find challenging to penetrate. For example, communicating your limits and avoiding negative interactions can protect you from bullying.

Asserting Authority

Vampires: Religious symbols repel vampires.

Covert Bullies: Asserting one's authority and confidence can repel covert bullies. Displaying self-assuredness and integrity is a holy symbol, clearly showing that covert bullying will not be tolerated. Demonstrating assertiveness in meetings and interactions shows that you are a challenging target.

Documenting Incidents

Vampires: Holy water burns and harms vampires, causing significant damage.

Covert Bullies: Keeping logs of incidents, including dates, times, and descriptions, provides vital evidence when reporting the covert bully.

Confrontation

Vampires: Driving a stake through the vampire's heart is a definitive way to kill it.

Covert Bullies: Directly addressing the covert bully and confronting their behavior can end it. Straightforward and assertive confrontation acts like driving a stake through the heart of the problem, showing that covert bullying will not be tolerated. Confronting the bully with specific examples of their behavior can help stop them.

Separation

Vampires: Beheading a vampire ensures it cannot rise again.

Covert Bullies: Cutting ties with the covert bully or creating physical and emotional distance can prevent further clandestine bullying. Removing oneself from the toxic environment or limiting interaction acts like decapitation, ensuring the bully has no further influence. That could mean minimizing contact, setting firm boundaries, or, in severe cases, distancing oneself from the toxic family member altogether.

Professional Help

Vampires: Exorcisms expel the vampire's spirit or curse.

Covert Bullies: Seeking professional help from therapists or counselors can expel the psychological impact of bullying. Professional guidance acts like exorcism, helping the target regain mental and emotional strength. Therapy can offer coping techniques and strategies to manage stress and trauma resulting from clandestine bullying.

Creating a Safe Environment

Vampires: Protecting the grave with objects prevents the vampire from rising.

Covert Bullies:

Supportive Home: Creating a supportive and safe home environment prevents the bully from having power. Positive, respectful surroundings make it difficult for covert bullying behavior to take root. Establishing a family culture of respect and open communication can discourage bullying.

Vigilance Matters: Paying attention to details and noticing subtle signs of bullying can prevent it from escalating. Vigilance and awareness of micro-facial expressions to keep bullying behavior in check. Observing interactions and being mindful of changes in behavior can help identify early signs of bullying.

Reflecting Behavior

Vampires: Vampires lack a reflection, and mirrors can identify them.

Covert Bullies: Covert Bullies: By mirroring the covert bully's energy and behaviors, you can observe how they react, revealing their true intentions. Responding to their actions with similar intensity and tone allows you to gauge whether their behavior is intentional or manipulative, providing insight into their underlying motives.

Collective Vigilance

Vampires: Communities keep watch during the night to guard against vampires.

Covert Bullies: Collective vigilance and support within a family can guard against clandestine bullying. A supportive network provides protection and intervention. Regular check-ins and discussions about family dynamics can help identify and address covert bullying.

Sharing Knowledge

Vampires: Sharing knowledge about vampire weaknesses helps communities prepare.

Covert Bullies: Teaching family members about the signs and strategies of covert bullying helps prepare and safeguard potential targets. Sharing this knowledge empowers relatives to identify and counteract bullying through community education. Family discussions and workshops on familial covert bullying awareness equip members with the skills to recognize and manage bullying effectively.

Unified Actions

Vampires: Communities work together to fight vampires.

Covert Bullies: Unified actions and collective responses within a family can effectively counteract clandestine bullying. A united front acts like a family effort, demonstrating that bullying will be addressed and stopped. Forming family support groups or committees to address bullying issues can strengthen the stance against such behavior.

Modern Interpretations

Utilizing Technology:

Vampires: Modern vampire stories use scientific approaches to find weaknesses.

Covert Bullies: Technology and modern tools, such as family communication apps like and documentation methods such as recording or videos, offer a safe and effective way to address and document familial clandestine bullying. These tools can be used to report, record, and track incidents within the family, making it more difficult for the covert bully to deny or gaslight their target. This can help prevent manipulation and hold the bully accountable.

Innovative Strategies

Vampires: Combining traditional methods with modern techniques provides innovative ways to combat vampires.

Covert Bullies: Similarly, blending traditional confrontation and support strategies with modern approaches can effectively counter covert bullying. Integrating old and new methods, this hybrid approach ensures more comprehensive protection. Combining psychological support with family agreements or rules creates a strong framework to defend against covert bullying, fostering empowerment in the process.

FAMILY DYNAMICS OF
VAMPIRES AND THEIR HOSTS

The Family Vampire

The Nocturnal Nature of Covert Bullying

The nocturnal nature of vampires is a compelling metaphor for the secretive modus operandi of covert bullies. Just as vampires emerge in the darkness, covert bullying typically takes place away from the public eye, where manipulative acts can occur without detection. This hidden abuse is particularly insidious because it allows the bully to manipulate perceptions and sow doubt, all while maintaining a veneer of normalcy during daylight hours. In family settings, this might manifest as a sibling a relative or even a parent who undermines a family member in subtle, often deniable ways or as a constant undercurrent of emotional abuse that chips away at the target's self-esteem and independence.

The dark cloak of night metaphorically shields these actions, allowing the bully to operate undetected and unchecked. The connection between the nocturnal activities of vampires and the covert operations of family bullies underscores the depth of the deception involved in such dynamics. It is this veiled nature of bullying that makes it particularly difficult to confront and resolve, requiring targets and supportive family members to be especially vigilant and proactive in recognizing and addressing signs of abuse.

Understanding and exposing the dynamics of covert bullying within families is crucial for breaking the cycle of abuse. Recognizing these behaviors as predatory and parasitic can empower targets and their allies to take decisive action, safeguarding the emotional and psychological well-being of all family members involved.

PARTICIPANTS IN THE COVERT BULLYING DYNAMIC

The Faminemy "The Familial Covert Bully". Orchestrates manipulation and control.

The Wannabe Bully: Aligns with the bully to avoid becoming a target.

The Bully's Target -"The Host": Bears the emotional burden of the abuse.

Covert Bullying Trio Dynamic

In the covert bullying dynamic, a toxic trio often emerges: the covert bully, the "wannabe" bully, and the target. At the center of this trio is the covert bully, or "the vampire," who manipulates and undermines others while hiding behind a facade of concern and charm. This behavior subtly drains the emotional energy of the target, gradually eroding their self-esteem and well-being. The covert bully shifts blame for family issues onto the target, leaving them burdened with guilt, anxiety, and a diminished sense of self-worth.

Further complicating the covert bullying dynamic is the presence of the 'wannabe bully,' a family member who aligns with the covert bully, often out of self-preservation rather than malice. This individual, who may be a sibling, cousin, or even a parent, joins in the bullying not because they are inherently malicious but to avoid becoming the next target or to secure their position within the family. They may engage in bullying behavior to gain favor with the covert bully or to deflect attention away from themselves. Unfortunately, by aligning with the covert bully, they unknowingly reinforce the cycle of manipulation and abuse, highlighting the role of each family member in preventing such dynamics.

The primary targets of familial bullying tend to be emotionally vulnerable individuals, particularly those who display sensitivity or empathy. Bullies exploit these traits, using covert tactics such as passive-aggressive remarks, emotional manipulation, and exclusion from family decisions. These strategies, applied over time, gradually drain the target's emotional reserves, leaving them feeling powerless and isolated. The long-term impact of covert bullying can be severe, affecting the target's mental health and overall well-being.

Targets span all age groups—from children who rely on their families for support to older adults who may require care later in life. Recognizing this broad spectrum is essential for creating support systems safeguarding their emotional well-being and dignity. Adding to the complexity is the pressure on marginalized family members to adopt similar toxic behaviors as a means of self-protection. This mirrors the allure of vampirism in folklore, a powerful metaphor for the appeal of toxic behaviors, where joining the predator offers protection from harm. In a family setting, engaging in manipulative behavior may appear to be a survival tactic, ultimately deepening the cycle of abuse.

Breaking free from this toxic dynamic requires recognizing the roles each participant plays. In this chapter, we explore the three key players in the covert bullying cycle: By understanding these roles, we can begin the process of healing from covert bullying, preventing its spread to other families, and fostering healthier, more supportive relationships.

The upcoming sections provide an in-depth analysis of the three main participants in the covert bullying triad. Exploring the psychological foundations of these roles provides strategies for breaking free from the cycle of covert bullying and reclaiming self-worth. Gaining insight into these hidden dynamics is the first step toward creating a brighter and more hopeful future.

THE FAMINEMY

Within the complex dynamics of family life exists a subtle yet destructive force known as the "faminemy"—a family member who engages in covert bullying rather than offering genuine love and support. This type of bullying functions through manipulation, psychological games, and a vampiric drain of emotional energy, gradually weakening the target.

The covert bully, "the vampire," orchestrates manipulation with charm and subtle tactics that conceal their true intentions. Meanwhile, the target, or "host," bears the emotional weight of the abuse, often becoming the scapegoat for the family's problems. However, by understanding and recognizing these tactics, individuals can begin to reclaim their power and address the issue.

In the following sections, we will delve deeply into the nature of the faminemy, exploring their tactics and psychological motivations.

The Jealous Sibling

 A sibling consumed by deep-seated jealousy often fears their sibling's success will overshadow their achievements. To prevent this, they engage in covert tactics such as gaslighting, targeting both their siblings and their sibling's children.

This envious sibling works quietly, undermining their sibling's confidence by planting seeds of doubt and insecurity. When their sibling accomplishes something significant, they quickly downplay the achievement, attributing it to luck rather than skill or effort.

They tarnish their sibling's reputation through subtle comments, attempting to diminish their standing within the family and community. As they grow older, the saboteur sibling extends their manipulative tactics to the next generation, targeting their sibling's children. Their goal is to perpetuate a cycle of sabotage, obstructing the children's chances for success. These actions deepen the fractures within the family, leaving the target's children confused and unsure of whom to trust.

By chipping away at their siblings' children's confidence and destabilizing family dynamics, the envious sibling aims to prevent their siblings' children from realizing their full potential. In conversations, the envious sibling often takes on a condescending tone, constantly striving to assert their superiority. During family gatherings, their subtle jabs and sarcasm are disguised as humor, concealing their true intentions.

Ultimately, the envious sibling is a silent saboteur, working behind the scenes to erode their sibling's self-belief and prevent them and their children from thriving. Driven by jealousy and insecurity, they resort to manipulation and gaslighting to maintain control. When confronted, they deny their actions, further distorting reality and perpetuating confusion and manipulation within the family.

The Jealous Relative

A jealous relative, driven by envy and the fear of being over-shadowed, can transform into a deceptive adversary within the family. Their envy fuels a covert campaign of manipulation and gaslighting aimed not only at undermining the target's success but also at extending their harmful influence to the target's children.

The manipulative tactics of the envious relative go beyond confrontation. They actively work to isolate the target by shaping the perceptions of family and friends and by casting doubts on the target's social competence. Their use of gossip and subtle character assassination is particularly damaging, as it tarnishes the target's social reputation, leaving them isolated and subject to ridicule.

The calculated cruelty they exhibit is chilling, as they seem indifferent to the emotional harm they cause. This behavior not only underscores the need for empathy and protection for the target but also exposes the envious relative's ruthlessness and disturbing lack of empathy. The long-term effects of this toxic influence can be devastating, affecting not only the target but also the broader family dynamic.

The Jealous Husband/Boyfriend

A husband is expected to provide support, love, and companionship in marital relationships. However, when jealousy infiltrates this bond, it can transform into a toxic and damaging dynamic. The jealous husband, driven by deep-seated insecurities and fears, may resort to covert bullying tactics to control and undermine his spouse. Unlike overt displays of anger or aggression, his jealousy manifests through subtle, insidious behaviors that gradually erode the wife's confidence and self-worth.

The jealous husband often employs manipulation, gaslighting, and emotional blackmail to keep his partner off balance and

dependent. He might disguise his jealousy as concern or love, making it difficult for his wife to recognize the malice behind his actions. His goal is to ensure that she never outshines him, going to great lengths to sabotage her opportunities for success. This can include character assassination, constant monitoring, unfounded accusations of infidelity, and isolating her from friends and family by tarnishing her image and credibility.

These behaviors create a sense of fear and uncertainty, ensuring that his wife remains within his control and never surpasses him in status. Such covert bullying can be profoundly damaging, leading to long-term emotional and psychological harm. The targets may find themselves doubting their perceptions and losing their sense of autonomy.

Friends and family may be unaware of the abuse, as the jealous husband often maintains a charming and respectable facade in public, reserving his manipulative tactics for private moments. Acknowledging the reality of the situation is the first step toward breaking free from the cycle of jealousy and manipulation.

By understanding these dynamics, targets can reclaim their independence, rebuild their self-esteem, and seek the necessary support to heal and move forward, achieving the goals they are meant to attain.

CHARACTERISTICS & PERSONALITY OF THE FAMINEMY

CHARACTERISTICS OF THE FAMINEMY

Predatory Nature

Identifying Vulnerable Family Members: Covert bullies excel at identifying family members they can manipulate, often testing their targets by applying subtle pressure to observe their reactions.

Persistent Exploitation: Once they identify the target, they persistently exploit that person, continuously attempting to dominate and control them.

Keen Observation: Covert bullies keenly observe behaviors and interactions, looking for signs of weakness and insecurities.

Targeted Attacks: They exploit these vulnerabilities by offering backhanded compliments and creating situations that reinforce the target's sense of inadequacy.

Fostering Tension and Unease

Covert bullies create an atmosphere of tension and unease within the family.

Indirect Control: They use indirect methods to exert control and cause harm, such as praising one sibling excessively while criticizing another.

Isolation Tactics: They spread rumors and manipulate family perceptions to isolate their target.

Emotional Vampirism

A faminemy generates continuous emotional demands and crises, forcing the target to constantly respond to their manipulations, leaving little time or energy for personal needs. Understanding the faminemy's cycle and tactics is crucial for recognizing and resisting the emotional drain they cause, ultimately paving the way to reclaim one's life.

Attempts to please and appease the faminemy often leave the target doubting himself and losing trust in his abilities. Recognizing this psychological dynamic involves understanding the manipulative patterns, acknowledging their impact on mental health, and seeking support from trusted individuals or professionals. This awareness is essential for breaking free and regaining control over his life.

Focusing on reclaiming personal goals and needs requires setting clear boundaries, engaging in individual therapy, and practicing consistent self-care. These strategies are vital to escaping the destructive cycle of manipulation, rebuilding confidence, and asserting autonomy over one's life.

PERSONALITY TRAITS OF THE FAMINEMY

Thriving on Emotional *Turmoil*: They amplify conflicts and insecurities, manipulating emotions to keep targets on high alert and in emotional distress.

Creating Dependency: By undermining the target's confidence and self-worth, covert bullies foster doubt and create a dependency where the target seeks the bully's approval and guidance.

Charming and Charismatic

Engaging Presence: Covert bullies often exude a magnetic personality that naturally draws people toward them. This engaging presence is a carefully constructed facade maintained by draining the energy of their chosen target.

False Confidence: By leveraging the target's energy, they project a false aura of strength and confidence, making them appear more charismatic to others.

Smooth Talker

Articulate and Persuasive: Covert bullies are adept at rationalizing their behavior and weaving compelling stories that portray them positively. This skill is most effective in the presence of their target, whom they use to bolster their image.

Feigning Innocence

Deflecting Suspicion: They present themselves as innocent or misunderstood, deflecting suspicion and playing the target to garner sympathy. This tactic helps them avoid accountability and maintain control over their narrative.

Calculating and Strategic

Meticulous Planner Meticulous Planner: Covert bullies carefully anticipate the consequences of their actions, thinking several steps.ahead and strategically timing their manipulations for maximum impact.

Observant: They have a heightened awareness of family dynamics, identifying alliance threats and monitoring reactions to adjust their strategies.

Adaptable: If a particular tactic stops working, they quickly pivot to new approaches, constantly refining their techniques to remain effective.

Addiction to Power and Manipulation

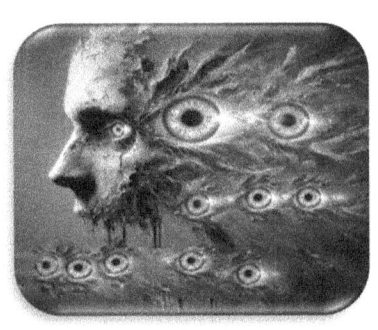

Often using their target as bait to gain more hosts.

Gaining Satisfaction from Distress

They derive pleasure from the pain and distress they cause, using emotional feeding and creating desperation to maintain control. They care solely about feeding their ego, disregarding the target's emotional well-being.

Escalating Manipulative Tactics

Their need for control leads to increasingly aggressive and sophisticated manipulative tactics. Their mind never rests in the pursuit of dominance.

Dependence on the Target: Their charm and charisma rely heavily on the target. Without this energy source, their captivating facade quickly dissipates, revealing their true nature.

****

TACTICS OF THE FAMINEMY

Gaslighting: A Symphony of Deception: -
Projection, Denial, and Deflection:
A Cycle of Manipulation

Faminemies project their negative traits onto the target, accusing them of the intentions and behaviors they themselves exhibit. This tactic allows the bully to portray themselves as the target and continue their covert manipulation without facing the consequences or being interrupted.

In addition to projection, faminemies use denial and deflection to evade responsibility further. They may deny wrongdoing, present different scenarios, or accuse the target of causing unnecessary trouble. By deliberately distorting reality through false information or outright denial of facts, they manipulate others' perceptions, causing the target to doubt their intuition, sanity, and judgment—especially when they are not believed. This results in confusion, self-doubt, and emotional turmoil, which significantly strengthens the bully's control over the target.

The impact of gaslighting on the target is profound and long-lasting. It gradually erodes the target's self-trust, distorts their perception of reality, and leads to isolation and invalidation. As the target internalizes these negative messages, they develop a deep sense of worthlessness. This manipulation often extends to the next generation, particularly the target's children. By distorting their reality, the covert bully ensures these children struggle to trust their instincts to succeed, effectively cursing future generations. This cycle of abuse sabotages the emotional well-being and prospects of future generations, dismantling trust within the family and perpetuating the bully's control.

Isolation, Alienation, and Triangulation

Faminemies isolate their targets within the family by spreading rumors and turning others against them. This tactic creates a profound sense of loneliness and vulnerability, leaving the target emotionally dependent on others for validation and support. By forming alliances with family members who are vulnerable to manipulation, faminemies strategically distort the family's perception of the target. This approach, often referred to as the "Engineering Division," amplifies the negative narrative about the target, further isolating them within the family dynamic.

Exploiting Idealism and Kindness

Covert bullies weaponize the target's idealism and kindness against their targets. They exploit the target's positive traits, using empathy and moral values to manipulate them and control the narrative. This tactic further confuses the target, as their best qualities are turned into weaknesses, making it even harder for them to recognize and defend against the abuse.

Employing Silent Treatment

They withdraw communication to create feelings of isolation and control, inducing anxiety and fear in the target.

Undermining Self-Worth

They subtly undermine the confidence and self-esteem of their targets through backhanded compliments, sarcasm, and veiled insults.

Creating Emotional Dependency

By undermining the target's confidence and self-worth, covert bullies foster doubt and create a dependency where the target seeks the bully's approval and guidance.

Thriving on Emotional Turmoil

hey create and amplify conflicts and insecurities, manipulating emotions to keep targets on high alert and in emotional distress.

Draining Emotional Energy

They constantly create emotional demands and crises, forcing the target to focus on solving these problems, as a result, the

target lacks time or energy to pursue their goals.

Sabotaging Efforts and Achievements

Covert bullies sabotage the target's efforts to achieve their goals by giving misleading advice and creating obstacles.

Character Assassination

Covert bullies engage in character assassination by spreading rumors and gossip to tarnish the target's reputation, damage their self-image, and respect from others.

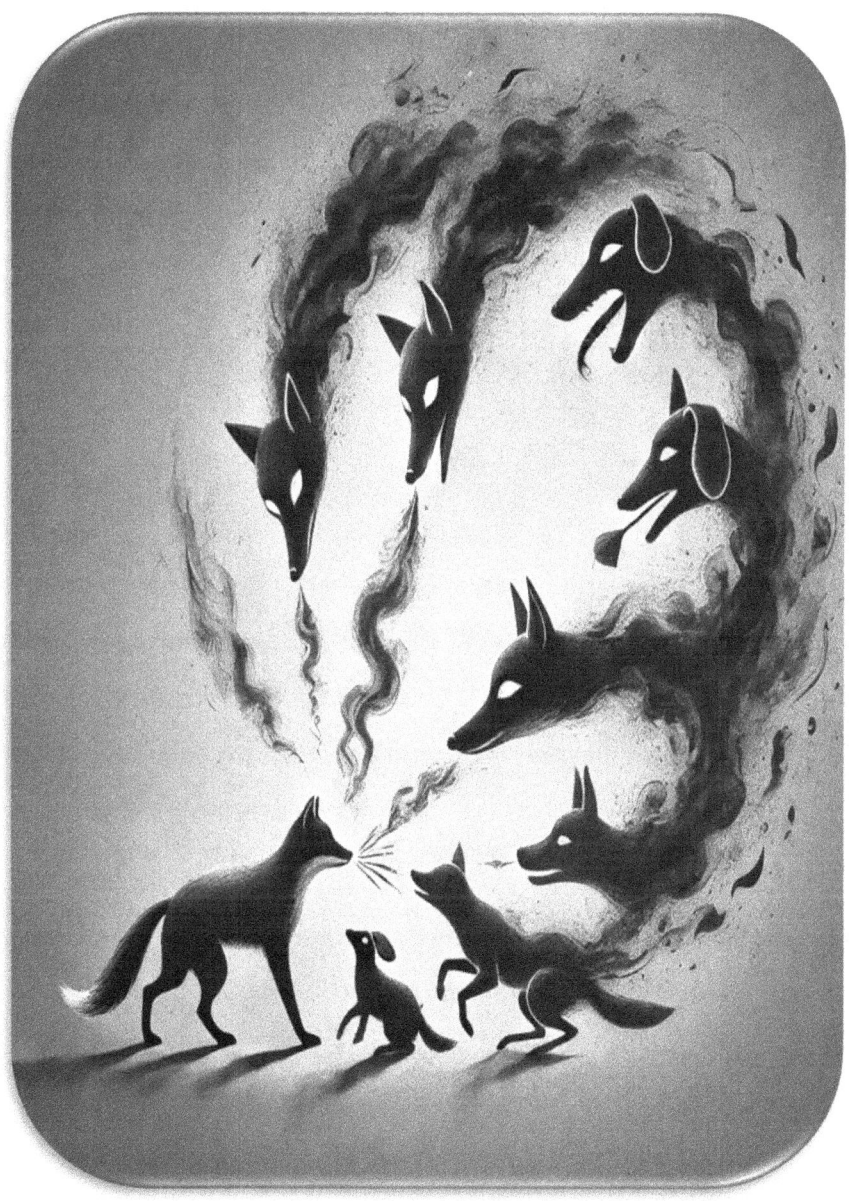

Perpetuating a Cycle of Abuse: Covert bullies actively involve their children in bullying the target's children, perpetuating a cycle of abuse across generations. They model disrespectful behavior, aggression, and manipulation, teaching their children to view the target's children as inferior or deserving of mistreatment.

Creating a Toxic Environment: These learned behaviors manifest in various forms of covert bullying, such as exclusion, ostracism, and spreading rumors, creating a toxic environment within the family.

Exploiting Personal Information and Betraying Trust

Covert bullies may weaponize personal information to manipulate and control their targets. By using sensitive details and exploiting the target's fears, they can manipulate emotions, often spreading rumors, half-truths, and lies to undermine the target's reputation and social standing.

Targeting insecurities and vulnerabilities strengthens the bully's hold, keeping the target trapped in a toxic dynamic that erodes their self-worth. Additionally, these bullies betray the target's trust by using personal secrets and intimate knowledge to gain an advantage. This exploitation deepens the target's emotional investment, making them more vulnerable to manipulation and control.

Dark Underbelly of Envy: Driven by jealousy, covert bullies use insidious tactics to sabotage the target's happiness and success. Through manipulation, gaslighting, and persistent subtle abuse, they create a toxic family environment that inflicts deep psychological wounds on the target. This behavior harms the individual and perpetuates a cycle of pain and suffering that can ripple across generations. It's crucial that we, as a collective, take action to break this cycle.

Subtle Scapegoating: Scapegoating involves subtle tactics like belittling smirks or mocking gestures to draw disrespect toward the target. This behavior diminishes the target's social standing and self-esteem while the covert bully maintains a facade of innocence or humor.

Contagious Nature: The covert bully subtly influences others to mimic their behavior, further perpetuating a cycle of disrespect and marginalization. Targets often struggle to recognize these actions as bullying, leading them to internalize the negative messages, which gradually erodes their self-worth.

Microaggressions: Discrimination within families often manifests as microaggressions, where subtle behaviors, attitudes, and verbal cues deliver derogatory or hostile messages to the target. These covert actions inflict deep emotional wounds that the target may feel too ashamed to discuss, allowing the covert bully to escape detection as the harm remains hidden beneath the surface.

Undermining, Discrediting: Familial covert bullies engage in a calculated and insidious strategy to undermine their target's reputation within the family. They do this by spreading rumors, half-truths, and lies that create doubt and suspicion, casting shadows on the target's character and diminishing their standing among relatives. At the same time, these bullies often discredit the targets by claiming credit for their ideas, contributions, and achievements. This not only positions them for recognition and acclaim within the family but also leaves the true architects of success in obscurity. The long-term effects of this covert bullying can be devastating, further eroding the target's self-worth and sense of accomplishment, and impacting their mental health and relationships.

Passive-Aggressive Behavior: Covert bullies often rely on passive-aggressive tactics such as backhanded compliments, sarcasm, or silent treatment to exert control and dominance. These behaviors, though challenging to confront directly, cause significant emotional distress for the target. By delivering veiled insults disguised as compliments, covert bullies undermine the target's self-worth and confidence while avoiding unwanted attention. Their subtle manipulation gradually erodes the Target's sense of self, making it difficult to challenge or address the abuse openly, highlighting the need for support and understanding in such situations.

Relational Aggression: Covert bullies employ social manipulation and exclusion to assert power and control over their targets, which often involves spreading rumors, gossiping, and forming alliances to ostracize specific individuals, isolating the target. Additionally, covert bullies use subtle put-downs, criticisms, and comparisons to undermine the target's self-worth. These tactics, though often difficult to detect, gradually erode the target's confidence and self-esteem, leaving them feeling diminished and isolated.

Guilt Tripping and Emotional Blackmail: Covert familial bullies often use guilt and emotional blackmail to manipulate their targets. For instance, they might make the target feel responsible for the family's financial problems or emotional distress, subtly shifting blame. This could be by saying things like, 'If you had done better in school, we wouldn't be in this mess or 'I'm sacrificing so much for you, and this is how you repay me?' This tactic fosters guilt and forces compliance, with the bully hiding behind a façade of concern or self-sacrifice, making it appears that the target's actions—or inaction—are causing harm to the family.

These bullies also use fear and shame to manipulate, eroding the target's sense of agency and compelling them to meet demands or conform to expectations. However, being alert to these tactics empowers targets to recognize the manipulation, reclaiming control and confidence in their lives.

Boundary Violations

Disregarding Boundaries: Intruding Privacy: Covert bullies often disregard or violate the target's boundaries to maintain control. They may intrude on the target's privacy, manipulate their possessions, or ignore their wishes, eroding the target's sense of autonomy.

Manipulation Through Flattery and Control

Covert bullies manipulate their target's circle through exces-

sive care, flattery, and sympathy to achieve compliance and control. By presenting themselves as caring and affectionate, they subtly erode the target's autonomy while reinforcing their power. This tactic fos-

ters emotional dependency, leading the target, plagued by self-doubt and diminished self-worth, to increasingly seek the bully's approval and guidance. Moreover, covert bullies feed off emotional turmoil, intentionally instigating and magnifying conflicts and insecurities. By trapping the target in a perpetual state of emotional distress, they assert control, ensuring the target remains dependent on them for emotional equilibrium.

COVERT TACTICS USED BY JEALOUS HUSBANDS

Controlling Information

The husband carefully controls the flow of information to mislead or confuse his partner, ensuring she makes decisions based on incomplete or false data. He may withhold crucial information or provide misleading facts to keep her in the dark. By distorting reality, he creates a narrative that makes her doubt her perceptions and decisions, effectively controlling her actions and thoughts without realizing them.

Gaslighting

A covert bully husband often employs gaslighting as a subtle yet powerful tactic to manipulate and control his partner. Gaslighting distorts reality and undermines the target's confidence, causing them to doubt their perceptions, memories, and even sanity. This psychological abuse allows the covert bully to maintain dominance while making the target feel increasingly dependent and insecure. Over time, the effects of gaslighting can lead to severe mental health issues and a complete loss of self-identity.

Master of Denial and Blame-Shifting: The husband is a cunning master of denial, consistently avoiding responsibility for his actions. When confronted, he shifts the blame onto his wife, making her question her own reality and sanity. Statements like, "You're overreacting," or "You're just imagining things" deflect accountability and allow him to maintain control. This insidious gaslighting further destabilizes her sense of reality, deepening his emotional manipulation, a fact that should outrage us and motivate us to act.

Emotional Blackmail: Using guilt as a weapon, he manipulates his wife into prioritizing his needs over her aspirations. He might say things like, "If you loved me, you would spend more time at home," making her feel guilty about pursuing her goals. He often portrays himself as the target to gain sympathy and control, deflecting attention from his manipulative behavior and making her feel responsible for his happiness.

Undermining Efforts & Sabotaging Opportunities

He actively interferes with his wife's professional opportunities, such as misplacing essential documents, giving her wrong information, or discouraging her from networking. He might offer backhanded compliments or sarcastic remarks that undermine her goals and make her feel inadequate, saying things like, "Are you sure you can handle that?" or "I don't think you're ready for that step."

Social Alienation

The husband isolates his wife from friends and family who might otherwise support her, making her increasingly dependent on him. He stirs up conflicts and spreads rumors to damage her reputation, ensuring that when she seeks help from mutual friends, they don't believe her and may even mock her. By sabotaging her relationships with mentors and colleagues, he leaves her isolated and unsupported, making it easier for him to maintain control. This behavior often leads the target to feel helpless and despairing.

Character Assassination

The husband spreads gossip through character assassination to tarnish his wife's reputation and credibility. He lies to mutual friends or colleagues, creating a false image of her that damages her social standing. Subtle public humiliations, like critical remarks made in front of others, further erode her confidence and self-image, intensifying the emotional abuse and reinforcing her sense of inadequacy.

Restricting Resources

The husband subtly controls or limits access to financial resources, making it difficult for his wife to pursue her goals. He deceitfully acts like he's struggling financially, encouraging her to help him manage the situation. By closely monitoring her spending and criticizing her financial decisions, he creates the illusion of concern while withholding money to prevent her from gaining financial independence. This economic control restricts her ability to make decisions and pursue opportunities freely while appearing as though he is simply trying to cope with financial challenges.

Passive-Aggressive Behavior

The use of the silent treatment creates feelings of isolation and anxiety, destabilizing her emotional well-being. He might refuse to speak to her for days, making her anxious and uncertain. Through passive-aggressive actions, such as misplacing essential items or intentionally neglecting tasks, he subtly sabotages her efforts and keeps her off balance.

Constant Criticism

Covert criticism of her appearance, intelligence, or capabilities erodes her self-esteem. Instead of delivering direct insults, he disguises his remarks as jokes, backhanded compliments, or "helpful advice." For example, he might say, "You looked nice in that dress last year," or casually mention how someone else handles a situation better. These veiled comparisons and passive-aggressive comments create feelings of inadequacy and competition. Over time, his constant stream of underhanded criticism wears down her confidence, causing her to doubt her worth.

Psychological Warfare

The husband exploits her insecurities by highlighting her flaws and weaknesses, keeping her in a perpetual state of self-doubt. He might focus on her past mistakes or failures, using them to make her feel insecure and incapable. By instilling fear of failure or abandonment, he makes her hesitant to take risks or pursue her ambitions, ensuring she remains under his control.

Denying Achievements

Despite the husband's attempts to belittle her, the wife's strength and resilience shine through. His jealousy leads him to undermine her achievements, with phrases like, "It wasn't that big of a deal," or "Anyone could've done that," that plant seeds of self-doubt. But she remains strong, her confidence unshaken. It's important to remember that your self-worth is invaluable and should never be compromised.

PARENTAL RIVALRY
JEALOUSY & COMPETITION

Envy and rivalry most commonly occur among siblings and married couples; these dynamics can occasionally surface in parent-child relationships. Although rare, this behavior is often generational, passed down from parents who were the targets of similar treatment. Driven by deep-seated insecurities, these parents may view their children as rivals rather than individuals to nurture and support.

This shift in perspective can lead them to subtly undermine their children's growth and success, planting seeds of self-doubt and insecurity. When envy takes root in the parent-child relationship, its impact can be profound and long-lasting, significantly affecting the child's well-being well into adulthood. The long-term effects can include diminished self-esteem, a distorted self-perception, and a reliance on external validation, all of which can hinder the child's personal and professional growth.

Jealous Mothers

Youth and Attention'

As their daughters blossom into youth and beauty, some mothers find themselves grappling with feelings of jealousy and insecurity.

It's important to approach these mothers with understanding and empathy, recognizing that their jealousy often stems from a fear of losing attention or being overshadowed by their daughters' vibrancy and success. By fostering a sense of compassion, we can begin to break the cycle of jealousy and competition in parent-child relationships.

In this toxic dynamic, the mother may compete with her daughter to maintain her status as the most attractive or charismatic woman in the household. She might make dismissive or critical remarks about her daughter's appearance, choices, or character, aiming to undermine her daughter's physical and emotional confidence. This behavior is often disguised as well-meaning advice or "tough love," making it difficult for the daughter to recognize it as covert bullying fueled by jealousy, even though she sensed something was wrong. The daughter is left grappling with a complex love-hate relationship with her mother, torn between seeking her approval and feeling undermined by her.

Examples of jealous Behavior in Mothers

Subtle Criticism of Appearance

A mother with a jealous nature may exhibit subtle criticism of her daughter's appearance, often cloaked in seemingly supportive remarks. For instance, she might say, 'That dress would look better if you had a different body type,' or, 'I had all the guys chasing me when I was your age.' Such comments subtly undermine the daughter's confidence, emphasizing the fleeting nature of youth and beauty. Additionally, the mother may highlight her own supposed superiority by asserting that, despite her daughter's physical attractiveness, she herself possesses greater charisma or style, often attributing this to her life experience.

Competing for Attention

In social situations, a jealous mother may actively redirect attention toward herself whenever her daughter receives compliments or recognition. She might behave in an overly youthful manner around her daughter's male friends or exaggerate her attractiveness and flirtatious behavior to keep the spotlight on herself. For instance, if someone praises the daughter's success at work or her appearance, the mother might interrupt with a story about her past achievements or how she looked in her youth, overshadowing her daughter's moment. Additionally, she may frequently interject in her daughter's conversations to shift the focus back to her own experiences or accomplishments.

Discouraging Opportunities

An envious mother might discourage her daughter from pursuing opportunities that could lead to success, often under the guise of protecting her. She might say, "You shouldn't go for that promotion; it's too stressful for someone your age," or "Don't waste your time chasing dreams that will never come true." The underlying message is that the daughter shouldn't aim too high lest she surpass her mother's life achievements.

The Impact on the daughter

Self-Gaslighting and Self-Doubt: The daughter suffers from confusing feelings that leave her feeling torn, she often feels conflicted between her deep desire for her mother's approval and persistent self-doubt. She struggles to trust her instincts and perceptions. This internal conflict can lead to self-gaslighting, a psychological term that refers to the process of doubting one's own thoughts, feelings, and experiences. In the context of parental envy, self-gaslighting can manifest as the daughter begins to question her abilities, attractiveness, or her right to seek success and recognition. As she experiences self-gaslighting, her self-perception becomes distorted, her confidence wanes, and she increasingly relies on external validation. This struggle can severely impact her inner sense of direction, leading to emotional and professional stagnation and limiting her potential in all aspects of life.

Competitive Fathers

Fathers who bully their or over Intelligence are, either because they feel threatened by the idea that their children might outshine them or because they genuinely believe their children cannot succeed and they are not as good as them. They may engage in both subtle and direct forms of bullying, frequently telling their children they are "not smart enough" or that they "will never measure up." While this behavior is similar to that of envious mothers, it typically centers around intellect rather than physical appearance. However, in some cases, fathers with their insecurities about aging or attractiveness might even find themselves competing with their sons in terms of physical appeal.

Examples of Competitive Behavior in Fathers Constant Undermining

Some fathers consistently belittle their children's intelligence and downplay their academic or professional achievements, using cut remarks to undermine their confidence and sense of accomplishment. For instance, they might say, "You think you're smart now, but wait until you face the real world," or "You only got that job because they were desperate enough to hire anyone." These comments are to deflate the child's self-esteem and convey that their efforts are not truly valued or deserve praise.

Often, this behavior stems from the father's insecurities and need for competition, where he feels the need to assert his superiority by targeting his child because he lacks the courage to compete with his peers. This constant belittling creates an environment where the child can never measure up or aspire to anything more significant, trapping them in a cycle of self-doubt and diminished self-worth.

Comparisons to Themselves

A common tactic of competitive fathers is to measure their child's achievements against their past successes, often casting themselves far superior at the same age. They might say things like, "When I was your age, I already had my own business up and running," or "I could solve problems like this in my sleep; you need to work harder if you ever want to catch up to me."

These comparisons aim to establish the father's superiority and reinforce his dominance, trapping the child in an endless cycle of trying to prove their worth. This relentless pressure often leaves the child feeling inadequate, as if no matter how much they achieve, it will never be enough to meet their father's standards.

In more personal areas, especially regarding romantic interests, the father might take the competition further by ridiculing his son with comments like, "You're not cool enough to handle a beautiful woman," or "You'll never attract anyone worthwhile acting like that." These degrading remarks not only belittle the son's intelligence and abilities but also undermine his confidence in social and romantic situations, deepening his sense of self-doubt.

Mocking Their Efforts

When children express their interests or ambitions, especially in creative or intellectual pursuits, some fathers react with mockery or sarcastic criticism. For instance, if the child eagerly shares a new idea or project, they're passionate about, the father might respond dismissively, saying, "That's cute, but you should leave the thinking to the real experts," or "You honestly believe that's going to work? Good luck with that." This kind of response strips the child of their enthusiasm, instilling a sense of inadequacy and discouraging them from taking risks or exploring their true potential.

The father's ridicule doesn't just dampen the child's motivation—it creates a deep-seated fear of failure and rejection, making the child hesitant to pursue their goals or express their ideas in the future. This pattern of competitive behavior in fathers can impact a child's psychological and emotional development.

Children raised under these conditions often struggle with self-worth, feeling that no matter their achievements, it will never be enough to earn their father's respect or approval. The constant need to prove themselves creates a heavy burden that can follow them into adulthood, affecting their personal and professional confidence. The competitive father's undermining behavior not only stifles the child's potential but also shapes their belief that they are destined to fall short of their goals.

BREAKING THE CYCLE

For daughters and sons to truly heal, they must abandon the idealized image of motherhood and fatherhood, seeing their parents as human beings with their flaws, pains, and vulnerabilities. Recognizing that their mothers and fathers may have never received the emotional support or psychological nurturing they needed during their upbringing helps them understand that their parents' behavior is often a result of unresolved insecurities. This shift in perspective allows the child to break free from the toxic cycle of competing with or seeking validation from their parents.

Compassion becomes the key to healing rather than holding onto anger and resentment. Accepting their parents as imperfect individuals with their struggles enables these children to move forward. Harboring anger will only trap them in bitterness, preventing their personal growth and prolonging their emotional pain. Breaking free from these harmful patterns means recognizing how their parents' insecurities have shaped their self-perception and learning to reclaim their sense of worth independent of these influences.

Parental competitiveness, though relatively rare compared to similar dynamics among siblings and married couples, is a significant issue that warrants attention. Its potential to damage family relationships highlights the importance of addressing it.

Acknowledging that parents are not merely idealized figures but flawed individuals with unresolved issues is a crucial first step in breaking the cycle. Recognizing the lasting impact of parental rivalry, which can hinder healthy emotional development, emphasizes the importance of addressing these patterns to ensure a positive emotional environment for the children and the family.

Addressing these dynamics not only empowers sufferers to confront external challenges and hidden adversaries but also opens up a world of potential for personal growth. Recognizing that manifesting success and self-worth requires overcoming visible and invisible obstacles is a journey that can guide them toward genuine personal growth. By highlighting the impact of envious parents, this section helps readers identify how subtle sabotage can hinder their potential, offering strategies to break the cycle of self-doubt and achieve their true capabilities.

THE FRENEMY

NAVIGATING THE COMPLEXITY OF FRENEMIES EMBRACING CLARITY AND CONFIDENCE

A frenemy is someone who outwardly appears to be a friend but secretly harbors feelings of hostility, jealousy, or a strong desire to compete. This dual nature—offering support while subtly undermining—makes identifying frenemies difficult. They present themselves as friends while quietly working against the person they envy, leading to confusion, self-doubt, and emotional distress.

The constant oscillation between acts of kindness and sabotage can be mentally exhausting and damaging to one's self-esteem. In such relationships, it's essential to maintain clarity and confidence to protect your well-being. By understanding the characteristics and behaviors of frenemies, we can equip ourselves to recognize and address these toxic dynamics effectively.

Recognizing & Addressing Frenemy Relationships

A Crucial Step. Frenemies pose a significant danger because they hide their true intentions behind a facade of friendship. Unlike apparent adversaries, they blur the lines between support and betrayal, making it difficult for their targets to understand the extent of the harm they cause. To effectively recognize and address these toxic relationships, it is essential to understand the psychology driving a frenemy's actions: deep-seated insecurities, a desire for control, and a fear of rejection often fuel frenemies.

Jealousy and competition are central to their behavior, influencing how they interact with those they perceive as rivals. Recognizing these underlying motives can help navigate and mitigate the negative impact of a frenemy in one's life. Armed with this knowledge, we can be more determined and motivated to identify and address such relationships, fostering healthier, more supportive environments.

Frenemies Not Always Women

Frenemies are not always women. While the term "frenemy" is sometimes stereotypically associated with female relationships due to cultural narratives, the phenomenon can occur between individuals of any gender. Frenemies exist in both male and female relationships, as well as in mixed-gender friendships.

The dynamics of a frenemy relationship are not exclusive to any gender. Men, women, and non-binary individuals can all experience and engage in these relationships. While the way these dynamics play out might differ based on socialization and cultural expectations, the core behaviors of a frenemy can be found in anyone. This understanding can help us feel less isolated and more understood in our experiences, knowing that these toxic dynamics are not unique to us.

Characteristics and Behaviors of a Frenemy

Insecurity and Jealousy:

Frenemies may feel inadequate or believe they deserve more than their friends, leading them to view their "friend" as a threat. This insecurity breeds jealousy, driving them to undermine their friend's success. Instead of celebrating their friend's achievements, a frenemy might diminish them through subtle criticisms or backhanded compliments intended to sow doubt.

Silent Rivalry:

For frenemies, life is a constant competition where someone else's success feels like a threat to their own. This mindset pushes them into a covert rivalry, where they seek to outdo or diminish their friend's achievements. Unlike healthy competition, a frenemy's competitiveness is destructive, fueled by a desire to see the other person fail.

Need for Control:

Frenemies may strive to assert control in relationships to feel more secure. This desire for dominance can manifest in manipulative behaviors, where they subtly steer their friend's decisions or actions to maintain influence over them, creating a power imbalance that keeps the other person dependent and uncertain.

Fear of Rejection:

Despite their negative behavior, frenemies often fear losing the relationship. They cling to the friendship out of fear of rejection, a need for someone to envy, or a worry that their friend might succeed without them. This paradoxical craving for approval and validation creates a complex emotional struggle that further complicates the relationship.

Cognitive Dissonance:

Frenemies experience cognitive dissonance, holding conflicting feelings of affection and resentment toward their friends. This internal conflict results in erratic behavior, where the targeted friend alternates between kindness and sabotage. The targeted friend, in turn, also suffers from cognitive dissonance as they struggle to reconcile the positive aspects of the friendship with the harmful ones. This confusion leaves the friend grappling with mixed emotions, making it even harder to recognize and break free from the toxic relationship.

Behaviors of a Frenemy

Backhanded Compliment:

A frenemy often disguises insults as compliments. These remarks, which may initially seem flattering, are intended to make the other person feel insecure or inadequate. For example, a frenemy might say, "You're brilliant for someone who didn't go to a top school," or "It's impressive you got that promotion, considering your experience." These comments subtly undermine confidence while appearing supportive.

Excessive Fake Flattery:

Frenemies often shower their friends with exaggerated, insincere praise, using it as a tool to manipulate the friend's perception of the relationship. This over-the-top flattery, which is often insincere, serves to keep the targeted friend complacent and under control. The frenemy subtly undermines their friend, using excessive compliments as a way to influence their actions and later sabotage them, highlighting the role of these compliments in their manipulation.

Gossip and Backstabbing:

Frenemies often gossip or backstab, sharing personal information or spreading rumors to damage the other person's reputation. They maintain a friendly front while quietly  working to discredit their friend. This behavior isolates the target and elevates the frenemy's status within their social circle.

Unreliable Support:

Frenemies enjoy maintaining a facade of support, finding satisfaction in their friend's struggles. They may offer help when it serves their interests, but they are likely to vanish or make excuses when their friend genuinely needs assistance. This unpredictability fosters instability and mistrust, leaving the person wondering whether they can rely on the frenemy.

Subtle Sabotage:

Frenemies are skilled at undermining others in ways that are difficult to detect. They might give bad advice, downplay their friend's achievements, or introduce doubt into the target's decisions. This sabotage often comes under the guise of concern or helpfulness, making it harder to recognize and address.

Inconsistent Behavior:

Frenemies are notorious for their unpredictable behavior. They may be warm and supportive for one moment, then distant or passive-aggressive for the next. This erratic behavior keeps the target constantly guessing about the status of the relationship, leading to anxiety and insecurity.

Undermining Achievements:

Instead of celebrating their friend's successes, frenemies often diminish them. They might say things like, "It's nice that you got the promotion, but I heard it wasn't that competitive," or "Anyone could have done that with the right connections."

These comments make the target feel less accomplished and more dependent on the frenemy for validation.

Constant Comparison:

Frenemies frequently compare themselves to their friend, constantly measuring their success against the other person's. This constant comparison fuels their insecurity and drives their need to undermine the other person. The frenemy might belittle their friend's achievements or choices, often under the guise of offering advice or sharing their experiences.

Boundary Violations:

Frenemies often push or ignore boundaries, whether they are emotional, physical, or social. They may intrude into personal matters, demand excessive attention, or disregard their friend's comfort levels. This behavior creates a sense of dependency in the friend, making recognizing and escaping the toxic dynamics challenging.

The Danger of Frenemies

Emotional Drain:

Frenemies are emotionally draining, constantly shifting between a facade of support and subtle sabotage. This unpredictability fuels anxiety and uncertainty, leaving the individual drained as they struggle to manage the relationship. As time passes, the emotional toll can result in stress, burnout, and potential physical health problems.

Undermined Self-Esteem:

A frenemy's subtle, consistent undermining can severely erode self-esteem. Targeted friends may begin to internalize the frenemy's criticisms and doubts, leading to a diminished sense of self-worth, which makes them more vulnerable to manipulation and further entrenches them in a toxic relationship.

Isolation:

Frenemies often isolate their targeted friend by driving wedges between them and others. They may spread rumors, create misunderstandings, or subtly discredit the person within social circles. This isolation deepens the friend's dependence on the frenemy, making it harder to recognize the toxic dynamics or seek outside support.

Psychological Exhaustion:

Recognizing the psychological manipulation of frenemies is crucial, as it often masquerades as genuine friendship. By exploiting the target's vulnerabilities and creating the illusion of mutual care, frenemies subtly influence and control their decisions, leaving the target emotionally drained. This manipulation erodes trust in others and damages the target's ability to form healthy, supportive relationships.

Awareness of these tactics empowers individuals to regain control and protect themselves from such toxic dynamics.

Over time, the uncertainty and emotional strain caused by a frenemy can lead to chronic stress. The constant need to remain vigilant and decipher mixed messages creates a toxic environment that erodes both mental and physical health. If left unaddressed, this ongoing stress may result in anxiety, depression, insomnia, and even more severe long-term health issues.

Sabotaged Opportunities

Frenemies often sabotage their friends' career opportunities, relationships, or personal growth. They may offer lousy advice, spread false information, or subtly discourage their friends from pursuing beneficial opportunities. The individual may repeatedly struggle, unaware that someone they trust is orchestrating their setbacks.

Rumor-Spreading with an Innocent Face

One of the most dangerous tactics of a frenemy is their ability to spread rumors while maintaining an innocent and friendly demeanor. They may quietly plant seeds of doubt or misinformation, all while appearing concerned or supportive. This duality allows them to sabotage others without raising suspicion, making them especially dangerous.

The Commonality of Frenemies

Normalization of Frenemy Behavior

In many social settings, frenemy behavior has become increasingly visible but often inadequately addressed. The distinction between friends and rivals frequently becomes blurred in competitive environments like schools, workplaces, and social media. This normalization enables toxic behaviors to continue unchecked, fostering a culture where mistrust and manipulation thrive.

Social Media Amplification:

Social media has intensified the presence of frenemies by fueling comparison and competition through curated, idealized portrayals of success. These platforms allow frenemies to subtly undermine others, often through passive-aggressive comments, exclusion from events, or carefully crafted posts intended to evoke envy and self-doubt.

Cultural Acceptance:

In some cultures, frenemies are seen as an unavoidable part of life or even a rite of passage. Unlike clear enemies, frenemies operate in the gray area between friend and foe, making their harm more insidious and harder to recognize. While the phrase 'keep your friends close and your enemies closer' encourages strategic vigilance against known adversaries, its misapplication to frenemies can lead to tolerating toxic relationships under the guise of necessity, which makes it even more challenging to acknowledge the need to distance oneself from such harmful connections.

Denial and Minimization:

Many people are in denial about the presence of frenemies in their lives. They may minimize the behavior, convincing themselves that the frenemy is just being "honest" or "competitive." This denial often stems from a fear of confrontation or a desire to maintain social harmony, even at the cost of one's well-being.

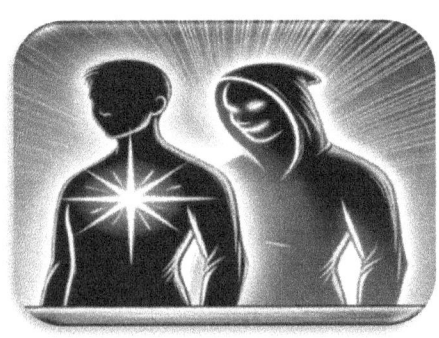

Stealthy Star:

The compulsion to be better than a close friend drives them to great lengths to sabotage anyone they perceive as threatening their status. Frenemies often need someone to envy because it gives them a sense of purpose and motivation. This creates a toxic relationship in which the frenemy constantly seeks to outdo their friend, not out of a desire for mutual success but to satisfy their need for superiority. This need to be the star can lead to sly behaviors, where the frenemy actively works to sabotage their friend's opportunities, reputation, or happiness.

The Widespread Impact:

The toxic influence of frenemy relationships is not confined to the individuals directly involved. It permeates through entire social circles, workplaces, and communities, creating an atmosphere of mistrust, competition, and manipulation. This behavior undermines collaboration, damages communication, and erodes mutual support, making it challenging for groups to achieve their goals and for individuals to thrive.

Recognizing and Breaking Free from Frenemies

Understanding the psychology and traits of a frenemy is crucial for identifying and managing these complex relationships.

Trusting your instincts, setting firm boundaries, and recognizing the warning signs are key to shielding yourself from the harmful effects of toxic dynamics. While frenemies may be more common than we realize, increasing your awareness and taking decisive action can minimize their negative impact and lead to healthier, more supportive connections.

It's common for the targeted friend to hold on to hope that a frenemy might change or that the friendship can be salvaged. And they may excuse their behavior, believing that with enough patience, the friend they once knew will reemerge. However, this hope is often misplaced. Frenemies typically follow deeply ingrained patterns of jealousy, competition, and manipulation, traits that are unlikely to change. Their actions reflect a consistent pattern of undermining others while pretending to be friends. No patience or effort can alter this fundamental aspect of their character, making it essential to recognize these behaviors and protect yourself from further harm.

It is crucial to recognize and address these toxic relationships to foster healthier, more supportive environments. By understanding the signs and dangers of frenemies, individuals can protect themselves from emotional and psychological harm. This awareness is the first step towards cultivating genuine friendships based on mutual respect, trust, and positive reinforcement, rather than competition and hidden animosities.

FAMINEMIES' AND FRENEMIES' EMOTIONAL DEPENDENCE ON TARGETS

The target plays a central role in the survival of the faminemy and frenemy. They rely heavily on the target to meet psychological and emotional needs that they are unable to fulfill themselves. This makes the target an indispensable element in maintaining their social facade and feeding their false sense of superiority.

Source of Psychological Energy:
The target serves as the primary provider of psychological energy for the Faminemy. By undermining the target's achievements or tarnishing their reputation, the Faminemy gains a false sense of superiority and control. This relationship is not reciprocal but built on emotionally and mentally draining the target, offering the Faminemy temporary relief that masks their internal fragility.

The Illusion of Superiority
Covert bullies often cling to a fabricated sense of superiority, masking a lack of genuine talent or creativity. This false narrative becomes their weapon of choice, aimed at eroding the confidence of their target—someone who embodies qualities that ignite envy in both *faminemies* and frenemies. By subtly undermining the target, these individuals strive to maintain

their self-deceptive perception of dominance, control, and superiority while concealing their insecurities.

Maintaining a Social Facade:

The Faminemy relies on the target to sustain their fake social image. The target's presence allows them to appear supportive and caring to others. Without the target, this facade quickly disintegrates, exposing their toxic nature.

Fear of Loss:

The Faminemy harbors an internal fear of losing the target, not only because they would lose their source of energy but also because the target's absence could expose their true nature to others. They rely on the target to justify their hostile behavior and shift blame, making the target's presence essential to sustaining their facade.

Crisis of the Faminemy When the Target Leaves

When the target recognizes the toxicity of the relationship and decides to distance themselves, the Faminemy enters a state of panic. This panic stems from their total dependence on the target as a source of psychological energy. The Faminemy may attempt to win the target back through emotional manipulation, pretending to change, or even resorting to threats. Their social facade and psychological stability hinge on the target's continued presence in their life.

Psychological Reflection:

The target becomes a mirror reflecting the Faminemy's insecurities and inner deficiencies. Yet, the Faminemy depends on this mirror to affirm their psychological identity, making the severing of this relationship devastating to them. Without the target, they experience a sense of emptiness and collapse. Understanding the Faminemy's Psychology: A Key to Liberation and Growth

The target often finds themselves bewildered and shocked by the depth of envy and manipulation exhibited by the Faminemy. This confusion arises from the target's empathetic and genuine nature, which makes it hard for them to grasp the Faminemy's psyche, driven by jealousy and fear of being outshined.

Letting Go of Confusion and Shock:

When the target realizes that this toxic dynamic does not reflect their worth or capabilities but is instead an expression of the Faminemy's inner void, they can break free from the confusion and self-doubt. This awareness can become a turning point toward emotional liberation.

Turning the Experience into Growth:

Recognizing the true nature of the relationship can serve as a catalyst for change. By ceasing attempts to understand or fix the Faminemy and accepting the toxicity of the relationship, the target can redirect their energy toward personal goals and success.

Confronting the Toxic Relationship: Awareness of the Dynamic:

Understanding their role in this relationship is the first step for the target to break free. Recognizing that they are being used as a psychological energy source makes them less susceptible to manipulation.

Releasing Guilt:

The Faminemy often uses guilt to keep the target tethered. Freeing oneself from this guilt is essential to regaining control over their life.

Building Self-Support:

The target must strengthen their social support network outside the toxic relationship, reducing the Faminemy's influence and creating space for healing.

Through this process, the target can achieve emotional and psychological independence, turning a painful experience into a valuable lesson that propels them toward greater personal and professional success.

UNDERSTANDING THE DYNAMICS OF COVERT AND OVERT BULLYING WITHIN FAMILIES

Bullying can manifest in various forms, with covert and overt bullying being two distinct yet interconnected behaviors. Understanding the interplay between these forms of bullying is crucial, as individuals who engage in clandestine bullying can also exhibit overt bullying tendencies and vice versa. This dynamic is particularly evident in romantic relationships, where overt bullying behaviors are often more pronounced.

Covert Bullying: The Hidden Manipulators
Characteristics and Behavior

Subtle, hidden behaviors that harm the target psychologically and emotionally characterize covert bullying. These behaviors include gossiping, spreading rumors, exclusion from social groups, backhanded compliments, and manipulating others against the target.

Covert bullies operate under the radar, making it difficult for the target and others to identify and address the bullying. The insidious nature of covert bullying means that the target often doubts their own experiences, feeling overly sensitive or paranoid. Covert bullies are deeply concerned with maintaining their image, usually presenting themselves as charming and likable individuals while causing significant damage to their targets. They thrive on the ability to harm others while appearing innocent, often leaving their targets isolated and unsupported.

Impact on Family Dynamics:

The insidious nature of covert bullying can erode family relationships from within. It creates a toxic environment where targets may question their perceptions and feel isolated. The psychological impact of such bullying is profound, as it can profoundly affect the self-esteem and mental health of family members, often leaving long-lasting emotional scars. Targets may experience anxiety, depression, and a pervasive sense of worthlessness. The subtlety of covert bullying makes it difficult to address, as the bully's actions are often disguised as concern or benign interaction, making it hard for targets to articulate their experiences or seek support. Covert bullies are rarely held accountable for their actions, making them more dangerous than overt bullies as they can continue their manipulative behavior without fear of punishment.

Overt Bullying: The Blatant Dominators in Romantic Relationships

Characteristics and Behavior:

Explicit, unmistakable acts of dominance and intimidation characterize overt bullies in romantic relationships. These acts might include verbal abuse, such as shouting, belittling, or name-calling; physical aggression, which could involve hitting, pushing, or other forms of physical violence; and visible controlling behaviors, such as dictating their partner's actions, isolating them from friends and family, or monitoring their activities.

Overt bullies do not hide their intentions and often use their dominance as a show of power to assert control over their partners. They thrive on the fear and submission they instill in their partners, believing that their overt aggression will maintain their authority within the relationship.

Impact on Romantic Relationships:

The presence of an overt bully within a romantic relationship can lead to a climate of fear, tension, and compliance. The bullied partner may feel compelled to conform to the bully's demands to avoid conflict, leading to a stifling atmosphere where open communication is curtailed. This environment can suppress individual expression and growth as the partner becomes overly cautious and submissive.

This dynamic can have profound long-term effects, including low self-esteem, anxiety, depression, and difficulty in forming healthy relationships in the future. Overt bullying is highly damaging, but overt bullies can often be held accountable and potentially face legal consequences, such as imprisonment. This possibility of punishment can act as a deterrent for overt bullies.

Why Covert Bullies Can't Be Overt Bullies and Vice Versa

Overt Bullies Lack Patience and Tactics

Overt bullies typically need more patience and nuanced tactics for covert bullying. Their approach is straightforward and aggressive, relying on explicit acts of intimidation and dominance to assert control. This direct method contrasts sharply with covert bullies' subtle and strategic manipulation. Overt bullies prefer immediate and visible results, and their impulsive nature makes it difficult for them to engage in the calculated and prolonged strategies necessary for covert bullying.

Covert Bullies Prioritize Social Image:

Covert bullies are deeply concerned with their social image and the perception of others. They go to great lengths to maintain a facade of kindness or neutrality while inflicting the most damage behind the scenes. They design their manipulative tactics to avoid confrontation and protect their public persona, ensuring they appear blameless or even benevolent. The fear of social repercussions prevents them from adopting the openly aggressive behavior characteristic of overt bullies, as they aim to come out "smelling like roses."

Personality Traits and Skills:

Covert Bullies: Covert bullies rely heavily on their ability to manipulate, deceive, and maintain a positive public image. They often possess traits such as cunning, patience, and subtlety. These individuals are adept at understanding and exploiting social dynamics without drawing attention to themselves. Their strength lies in their ability to harm others while appearing innocent, which requires high social intelligence and restraint.

Overt Bullies: Overt bullies thrive on confrontation and visible displays of power. They are typically more aggressive, confident, and unafraid of social or legal repercussions. Their bullying tactics are straightforward and intimidating, relying on physical strength or verbal aggression. These individuals often lack the subtlety and restraint necessary for covert bullying, as their primary goal is to assert dominance openly and immediately.

Public Image and Consequences

Covert Bullies: Maintaining a kind and positive public image is paramount for covert bullies. Their ability to manipulate and deceive relies on the

perception that they are trustworthy and likable. Engaging in overt bullying would risk exposing their true nature and dam-

aging their carefully constructed facade. The fear of social and professional consequences keeps them from cross-

ing into overt bullying territory.

Overt Bullies

Overt bullies are less concerned with their public image and more focused on asserting control through visible means. They are often willing to accept the risk of social and legal consequences because their primary goal is immediate dominance. Their behavior is blatant and aggressive, making it easier for them to adopt the subtle, hidden tactics of covert bullying with a significant shift in their approach and mindset.

Method of Control

Covert Bullies: The control exercised by covert bullies is psychological and emotional. They undermine their targets' confidence and social standing through indirect actions, ensuring their manipulation remains hidden. This method of control is slow and insidious, often leaving the target and others unaware of the true source of the distress.

Overt Bullies: Overt bullies control their targets through fear and intimidation. Their actions are designed to be seen and felt immediately, and they assert their power by using physical or verbal aggression. This direct control method is incompatible with the covert bully's need for secrecy and subtlety.

Context and Environment

Covert Bullies: Covert bullying often occurs in environments where subtlety is required, such as workplaces or social settings where open aggression would be socially unacceptable or professionally damaging. Covert bullies excel in these contexts because they can operate without drawing attention.

Overt Bullies: Overt bullying is more likely to occur in environments where the bully feels secure and less constrained by social norms, such as within intimate or familial relationships. The overt bully's tactics are direct and forceful, making them less effective in settings that demand discretion.

Interchangeability and Coexistence

Despite the challenges in switching between these forms, some individuals can exhibit both covert and overt bullying tendencies, depending on the context and their relationship with the target. For instance, a person who engages in covert bullying at work, where subtlety is required, may exhibit overt bullying behaviors at home, where they feel more secure in their power and less concerned about repercussions.

The ability to blend into different environments and adapt their tactics makes them particularly dangerous, as they can cause extensive harm while maintaining an unblemished public persona.

Psychological Traits of Bullies

Both covert and overt bullies share certain psychological traits, such as a need for control, a lack of empathy, and a desire to elevate themselves by diminishing others. These traits allow them to adapt their bullying tactics to different situations. However, their primary mode of bullying often reflects their core personality and preferred methods of manipulation or aggression.

Overt Bullying in Romantic Relationships

Over bullying behaviors are particularly prevalent in romantic relationships. In these intimate settings, bullies often feel more secure in their power dynamics and are less restrained by social norms and professional consequences. They may resort to overt tactics such as verbal abuse, physical violence, and overt control to dominate their partner. The familiarity and emotional closeness of romantic relationships provide fertile ground for overt bullying to thrive, as the bully exploits the emotional vulnerabilities and dependencies of their partner.

Impact on Targets

The effect of both covert and overt bullying on targets can be profound and long-lasting. Targets of covert bullying frequently experience depression, anxiety, and a reduced sense of self-worth because of the continual, subtle nature of the abuse. Those subjected to overt bullying experience fear, trauma, and physical harm, along with emotional and psychological damage. In romantic relationships, the combined effects of covert and overt bullying can lead to severe emotional distress, isolation, and a breakdown of the target's self-identity and independence. Recognizing the distinct nature of covert and overt bullying is essential for understanding the full spectrum of bullying behaviors.

While some individuals may exhibit both forms of bullying, they typically lean towards one primary method. By recognizing and addressing both covert and overt bullying, it becomes possible to more effectively support targets and create better strategies to prevent and combat all forms of bullying. The reality that overt bullies can face legal consequences, including jail time, for their actions, while covert bullies often evade accountability, highlights the insidious nature of covert bullying.

MODERN STORIES OF FAMILIAL CON-FLICT
A GLOBAL PERSPECTIVE

THE SAD PRINCESS

A prominent figure within a royal family became the target of covert bullying due to her sensitivity, beauty, and perceived naivety. Her genuine nature and emotional openness, which should have been celebrated, made her vulnerable to manipulation and exclusion.

The covert bullying she faced was insidious, often disguised as concern or formality, but its impact was devastating. She was subjected to emotional isolation, with her attempts to integrate into the family quietly undermined. Despite the quiet, calculated manipulation that preyed on her sensitivity, she showed immense courage. This manipulation eroded her confidence and self-esteem, but she continued to face it with strength.

The lack of open hostility made it difficult for her to confront the issues directly, leaving her feeling trapped and unsupported. Over time, this covert bullying caused significant emotional damage, contributing to severe mental health struggles, including depression and an eating disorder. The relentless strain of maintaining her public image while enduring hidden manipulation took a heavy toll, leading to profound emotional exhaustion and long-term psychological consequences. Her vulnerability, rather than being met with care, became the very reason she was isolated and undermined, leaving her to suffer in silence.

STORY OF A GLOBAL ICON

Covert bullying deeply affected the life of this global star, a vulnerable individual who captivated the world with his extraordinary talent as a singer and dancer. Despite his fame and success, he was relentlessly subjected to covert bullying, starting within his family. The constant pressure to perform and the emotional strain of being scrutinized chipped away at his self-worth. Though praised publicly behind closed doors he faced manipulation, belittlement, and criticism that left lasting scars.

With his rising fame, the intensity of covert bullying also escalated. The public, unaware of his childhood marked by emotional isolation and relentless pressure, ridiculed his eccentricities. The media, in a pretense of concern, sensationalized his every move, magnified mistakes, and questioned decisions. This cycle of public and private manipulation left him grappling with his identity and trust, a struggle that would persist.

The covert bullying extended to his relationships, where betrayals were common. Friends turned on him, using his vulnerabilities for their own gain. This deepened his isolation and reinforced the belief that he couldn't trust anyone. Despite his outward success, the emotional toll of this constant, subtle bullying and ridicule haunted him, making it a constant struggle to find peace or genuine happiness. after the world stops watching. The relentless manipulation and hidden abuse he endured, both privately and on a global scale, left profound psychological effects that never fully healed.

HISTORICAL ACCOUNTS OF FAMILIAL CONFLICT-*A GLOBAL VIEW*

Covert bullying has been a part of human interactions since the beginning of time. It is deeply embedded in human nature, manifesting in subtle yet damaging ways across cultures and eras. Ignoring or denying its existence allows covert bullies to thrive, making countless individuals prey to their manipulative tactics.

Ancient Civilizations

Queen Hatshepsut and Thutmose III (Ancient Egypt)

One of the most famous cases of covert bullying in Ancient Egypt is Queen Hatshepsut sidelining her stepson Thutmose III. As regent turned Pharaoh, she likely manipulated court officials and resources to maintain power for over two decades.

Ramses III's Harem Conspiracy:(Ancient Egypt)

Ramses III faced the Harem
Conspiracy, where his wife
Tiye covertly plotted to place
her son Pentawere on the
throne. Through manipulation
and covert bullying, she undermined his authority, lead-

ing to a failed coup, trials, and executions.

Agrippina the Younger and Nero:(Ancient Rome)

Agrippina, mother of Emperor
Nero, used manipulation to
control him, fueling paranoia
and violence. Her tactics led
Nero to order her murder, highlighting the harm of covert control.

Empress Lü Zhi: (Ancient China)

Lü Zhi, wife of Emperor
Gaozu, used covert tactics to
secure power, orchestrating
deaths and manipulating
court politics. Her actions
sowed fear and caused
lasting instability.

The Power Struggles of the Ptolemaic Dynasty (Ancient Egypt)

The Ptolemaic dynasty faced intense covert bullying, with Ptolemy VIII using rumors, manipulative marriages, and emotional tactics to secure power. His actions fueled family conflicts, causing political instability and weakening the dynasty's rule over Egypt.

Medieval Times

Eleanor of Aquitaine (Medieval Europe):

Eleanor of Aquitaine's manipulations fueled conflicts within her family, causing emotional strain and prolonged turmoil. Her actions deeply impacted the mental well-being of those involved.

RELIGIOUS NARRATIVES OF FAMILIAL CONFLICT ACROSS CULTURES

THE STORY OF CAIN AND ABEL

IN THE QURAN AND THE BIBLE

The story of Cain and Abel, as presented in both The Bible and The Quran, offers a timeless lesson on the dangers of jealousy, covert manipulation, and unchecked emotions. Cain's deep-seated envy and cunning behavior, driven by a profound sense of rejection, lead to a tragic and violent outcome that has resonated through the ages.

The Root of Cain's Jealousy

In The Quran

The Quran recounts a similar story of Cain (Qabil) and Abel (Habil). Both brothers offer sacrifices to God, but God accepts Abel's sacrifice while rejecting Cain's. The Quran emphasizes that God accepts offerings only from those who are righteous and sincere in their devotion. Abel advises Cain to rectify his ways rather than be consumed by jealousy. Despite this counsel, Cain's jealousy intensifies, driven by wounded pride and rejection. His failure to control these feelings ultimately leads to his decision to commit fratricide.

In The Bible

Although the Bible does not specify why God preferred Abel's offering, it implies that Abel made his sacrifice with a purer heart or greater devotion, while Cain's may have lacked sincerity or quality. Cain's failure to accept this rejection without harboring resentment leads to tragedy. In both traditions, Cain's jealousy begins subtly. God's perceived favoritism fuels his resentment towards Abel. This internalized envy and inadequacy remain hidden from others but grow more robust.

Cain's failure to confront his feelings or seek resolution allows these emotions to fester, laying the groundwork for his subsequent actions.

Rather than openly addressing his grievances, Cain resorts to covert manipulation. He invites Abel into the fields, a seemingly innocent request that masks his true intentions. Cain's act of deception plays a critical role in his manipulation. By luring Abel into a secluded area, Cain ensures that he can execute his plan to kill his brother without interference, all under the guise of a peaceful interaction.

The Murder and Its Divine Consequences

The culmination of Cain's covert bullying is the murder of Abel. This premeditated act is not just a spontaneous outburst of anger but the result of a calculated plan to eliminate his brother, whom he sees as a rival. The tragic outcome is the first murder in religious history, underscoring the lethal consequences of unchecked jealousy and manipulation.

Cain's killing of Abel marks the first instance of fratricide in religious texts. This act of violence, driven by jealousy and manipulation, highlights the destructive power of these emotions when left unchecked. The murder is not just a personal tragedy but a foundational event with profound theological implications, symbolizing the dangers inherent in harboring negative emotions.

Following Abel's murder, God confronts Cain, asking him where his brother is. When Cain attempts to evade responsibility, God reveals that Abel's blood cries out from the ground, signifying divine awareness of the crime. In both the Bible and the Quran, God punishes Cain, marking him and condemning him to a life of wandering and alienation. This punishment reflects the severity of Cain's actions and serves as a divine lesson on the consequences of jealousy and violence.

Impact on Cain

His actions irrevocably alter Cain's life. The weight of his guilt, combined with divine punishment, isolates him from his family and community. His existence becomes one of perpetual wandering, symbolizing the alienation and inner turmoil that result from his crime. However, if no one had discovered the crime, Cain might not have felt the same depth of guilt, as his jealousy was so overpowering that it eclipsed other emotions, including remorse.

This outcome serves as a stark reminder of the long-term repercussions of allowing jealousy and manipulation to govern one's actions. In some later Jewish and Islamic traditions, additional interpretations or folklore have expanded on the basic story, occasionally incorporating elements related to Cain and Abel's marriages or other familial dynamics. The idea that Abel's wife was more beautiful than Cain's is found in some apocryphal and Midrashic stories, suggesting that part of Cain's jealousy stemmed from a rivalry over a woman. While this aspect is speculative and not part of the core scriptures, it presents a valid reason for jealousy in these expanded interpretations, adding another layer to Cain's motivation and the resulting tragic outcome.

The story of Cain and Abel remains a powerful reminder of the profound consequences that can arise from allowing jealousy, covert manipulation, and unchecked emotions to fester. Although the narrative explicitly punishes the act of murder, it also highlights the destructive potential of unchecked jealousy, which can drive individuals to commit heinous acts. Ultimately, the story underscores the importance of confronting negative emotions and seeking resolutions before they manifest in destructive ways, ensuring that jealousy and resentment do not lead to irrevocable tragedy.

THE STORY OF JACOB AND ESAU
(JUDAISM, CHRISTIANITY, ISLAM)

The story of Jacob and Esau, found in the Torah and Bible and referenced in Islamic tradition, is not just a compelling example of how cunning and covert manipulation within a family can lead long-lasting and tragic consequences but also a significant religious narrative. Jacob, with the encouragement of his mother Rebekah, engages in a series of deceitful tactics to undermine his brother Esau and secure the birthright and blessing that were rightfully Esau's.

Cunning and Covert Manipulation
Early Deception

Jacob's manipulation begins subtly. One of the first instances is when he convinces Esau to sell his birthright for a mere bowl of stew. The birthright, which granted the firstborn son a double portion of the family's wealth and leadership, is given up by Esau in his impulsiveness and focus on immediate hunger. This act of selling The Birthright is a significant event in the story, as it sets the stage for Jacob's further deceitful actions.

Rebekah's Intricate Plan

Jacob's mother, Rebekah, plays a pivotal role in the deception. Favoring Jacob, she conspires with him to deceive Isaac, their father, who is old and blind. Re-bekah devises a complex

plan for Jacob to receive the blessing intended for Esau. She instructs Jacob to disguise himself with animal skins and Esau's clothing and prepares a meal to further deceive Isaac into thinking he is blessing Esau.

The Heartbreaking Deception

Jacob, disguised as Esau, approaches Isaac for the blessing. Isaac, believing he is blessing Esau, gives Ja-cob an irrevocable blessing that grants him authority over the family and divine favor. This deception de-prives Esau of his rightful in-heritance and leaves him

with a lesser blessing. Upon discovering the deceit, Esau's devastation underscores the profound emotional impact of Jacob's actions, evoking sympathy from the audience.

Tragic Outcomes: Lifelong Resentments

The immediate aftermath of the deception is profound. Esau reacts to the loss of his birthright and blessing with deep anguish and resentment, creating a lasting rift between the brothers. This betrayal fuels lifelong animosity, as Esau vows to kill Jacob, highlighting the severe emotional consequences of Jacob's deceit.

Family Division

The deceit causes long-term repercussions for the family. The division between Jacob and Esau affects their descendants and broader family dynamics, leading to ongoing strife and conflict across generations. This family division underscores the far-reaching effects of covert bullying and deceit.

Jacob's Fleeing

Fearing for his life, Jacob flees his home to escape Esau's wrath. His exile highlights the personal and familial costs of their deceitful actions, vividly illustrating the destructive power of manipulation.

Esau's Redemption and Reconciliation

Prosperity Despite Loss: Esau finds his path to success despite his significant losses. He becomes the father of the Edomites, a powerful and prosperous nation. Despite losing his birthright and blessing, his success demonstrates his resilience and ability to overcome adversity.

Reconciliation with Jacob

A significant moment in Esau's story is his eventual reconciliation with Jacob. After many years, Jacob returns home, fearing Esau's anger. He prepares gifts to appease Esau, but Esau embraces and forgives Jacob when they meet. This forgiveness heals a deep family wound and highlights the possibility of reconciliation after betrayal.

The story of Jacob and Esau illustrates the profound and far-reaching impacts of cunning and covert manipulation within familial relationships. Jacob's deceit, encouraged by Rebekah, results in lifelong resentment and division. Esau suffers significantly due to the loss of his birthright and blessing but ultimately finds prosperity and reconciliation. His story is a powerful reminder of the destructive power of deceit and the enduring possibility of redemption and healing within families.

THE STORY OF JOSEPH AND HIS BROTHERS (JUDAISM, CHRISTIANITY, ISLAM)

The story of Joseph and his brothers, as recounted in the Torah, Bible, and Quran, vividly demonstrates how jealousy and deceit can fuel cunning and covert bullying with tragic results. Joseph's journey unfolds through manipulations by his brothers and others who aim to exploit him.

Cunning and Covert Manipulation

Subtle Undermining: Joseph's brothers, driven by envy over the special affection their father Jacob shows him, begin their covert bullying through subtle undermining. They sow seeds of resentment and ill will against Joseph, creating an environment of discord and jealousy within the family.

Deceptive Plan

Fueled by intense jealousy, they first threw him into a dry well (or pit) after stripping him off his richly ornamented coat, symbolizing their father's favoritism.

This act is not just physical but deeply symbolic, as they seek to strip Joseph of his special status and dignity within the family. Later, upon seeing a passing caravan of Ishmaelites (or Midianites), they decide to sell Joseph into slavery for twenty pieces of silver. Their plan reaches its peak in a cruel deception: they dip Joseph's coat in goat's blood and present it to their father, Jacob, leading him to believe that a wild animal has killed his beloved son. This calculated deceit not only conceals their true intentions but also inflicts profound emotional trauma on their father, leaving a deep scar on the family.

The Cunning of Potiphar's Wife

After being sold into slavery in Egypt, Joseph's trials continue when he catches the eye of his master Potiphar's wife. She attempts to seduce him, but Joseph, being a man of integrity, refuses her advances.

Angered by his rejection, Potiphar's wife falsely accuses him of trying to assault her, leading to Joseph's imprisonment. This episode illustrates how, when one faces adversity, troubles often seem to come in waves, compounding one another unless one becomes aware and vigilant, as Joseph ultimately does.

Years of Suffering

Wrongfully imprisoned, Joseph endures years of hardship and separation from his family. His betrayal and the suffering that follows highlight the profound impact of covert bullying and manipulation. The emotional and psychological toll of being falsely accused and imprisoned deepens his anguish.

Long-Term Impact

The brothers' and Potiphar's wife's cunning manipulations set off a chain of events that affect Joseph, his entire family, and the broader society in Egypt. Ironically, Joseph's eventual rise to power brings his brothers back into his life during a time of famine. This reunion, marked by Joseph's forgiveness, underscores the enduring consequences of their initial actions.

Emotional and Familial Strain

The deceitful manipulation and emotional trauma inflicted on Joseph and his father led to lasting familial rifts. The story vividly illustrates how covert bullying and cunning manipulation, driven by jealousy and deceit can create profound and enduring emotional scars, affecting relationships and destinies for years to come.

The story of Joseph and his brothers and the betrayal by Potiphar's wife is a compelling example of how jealousy, deceit, and covert bullying can lead to significant and tragic outcomes. The subtle undermining, deceitful actions, and wrongful accusations Joseph faced resulted in years of suffering and emotional turmoil for both him and his father. This tale highlights the far-reaching consequences of covert bullying and the lasting impact of such actions on individuals and families while also showing how awareness and integrity can ultimately lead to redemption.

Joseph's Path: From Betrayal to Success & Forgiveness

Joseph's journey from adversity to success and ultimately to forgiveness is a remarkable testament to resilience, faith, and personal growth. His rise to power in Egypt was a pivotal turning point, yet his ability to forgive his brothers resulted from his resilience, deep understanding, and unwavering faith in divine purpose. Joseph's resilience in the face of adversity is truly inspiring. After being sold into slavery, Joseph's hard work and integrity earned him trust in Potiphar's household. However, a false accusation by Potiphar's wife led to his imprisonment. Joseph's character shone through even in prison, earning him favor with the prison warden. His divine gift of interpreting dreams led to his release when he correctly interpreted Pharaoh's troubling dreams, predicting seven years of abundance followed by seven years of famine.

Joseph's unwavering faith was a guiding light in his journey. Impressed by his wisdom and leadership, the Pharaoh appointed him second-in-command, tasking him with preparing Egypt for the coming famine. This position of power reunited Joseph with his brothers, who came to Egypt seeking food during the famine. Rather than seeking revenge, Joseph forgave them, understanding that their betrayal had ultimately been part of a greater plan. He famously told them, "You intended to harm me, but God intended it for good."

Joseph's story is a powerful testament to the healing power of forgiveness. His success allowed him the peace and perspective to reflect on his journey, recognizing how each trial shaped him into a leader. His forgiveness was born from his newfound power and his unwavering faith and trust in a larger purpose. In the end, Joseph's story highlights his perseverance, wisdom, and strength to forgive, showing that true success lies in power and the ability to rise above challenges while healing others.

The Story of Amaterasu and Susanoo
(*Shintoism*)

Cunning and Covert Manipulation, Jealousy and Disruption: Susanoo, driven by jealousy of Amaterasu's revered position as the sun goddess, employs several tactics to undermine her authority and disrupt her influence. His resentment leads him to take subtle yet destructive actions to diminish Amaterasu's status.

Defiling Sacred Spaces

Susanoo defiles Amaterasu's sacred spaces and destroys her rice fields. Though these acts are overt in their destructiveness, the intent behind them is not just the rice fields; he has a long-term goal. Susanoo aims to emotionally and psychologically torment Amaterasu, provoking a response that would weaken her standing.

Psychological Intimidation

Beyond physical destruction, Susanoo engages in psychological intimidation. His persistent efforts to undermine and humiliate Amaterasu are designed to break her spirit and challenge her authority indirectly.

Amaterasu's Withdrawal

The culmination of Susanoo's covert bullying leads Amaterasu to a profound emotional crisis. Overwhelmed by his relentless attacks and feeling isolated, she retreats into a cave, symboliz-ing her psychological defeat and plunging into the world into darkness.

Consequences of Darkness

The resulting darkness engulfs the world, illustrating the far-reaching and catastrophic impact of Susanoo's covert bullying.

The natural world suffers from the loss of light and warmth, demonstrating how personal grievances and covert manipula-tion can have devastating consequences for the broader.

Resolution: The gods eventually intervene and convince

 Amaterasu to emerge from the cave, restoring light and balance to the world. However, this episode serves as a powerful reminder of the severe emotional distress and widespread impact that can result from cunning manipulation.

The story of Amaterasu and Susanoo underscores how covert bullying, driven by jealousy and psychological manipulation, can lead to severe emotional distress and catastrophic out-come. Susanoo's actions, while partly overt, are rooted in cov-ert tactics aimed at undermining his sister, resulting in a period of darkness that affects both the divine and earthly realms. This tale highlights the destructive power of envy and the ur-gent need to address underlying conflicts before they escalate.

The Story of Osiris, Isis, and Set:

Covert Manipulation in Ancient Egypt

Jealousy and Envy: Set, the god of chaos and disorder, is consumed by jealousy towards his brother Osiris, who is beloved by the gods and revered by the people. This envy drives Set's desire to usurp Osiris's power and influence, leading him to devise a meticulously planned scheme.

Deceptive Invitation: Set's manipulation begins with a seemingly innocent gesture—a grand feast in honor of Osiris. He invites Osiris under the guise of celebration, using the opportunity to lower his brother's guard. Set's outward friendliness hides his true intentions, showcasing his cunning nature.

The Coffin Trap: During the feast, Set presents a beautifully crafted coffin as a gift and challenges the guests to see who fits inside. Knowing that Osiris, trusting his brother, will lie down in it, Set seizes the opportunity. Once Osiris is inside, Set quickly seals the coffin and throws it into the Nile River, ensuring Osiris's death without direct confrontation. This act of deception is a masterclass in covert manipulation, demonstrating how deceit can be used to execute a deadly plan under the guise of goodwill.

Tragic Outcome: Osiris's Death: Osiris's death directly results from Set's cunning plan. By eliminating Osiris in such a covert manner, Set removes his brother and destabilizes the Egyptian pantheon. Osiris's death brings chaos to both the divine and mortal realms.

Impact on Isis and the Divine Order

The tragedy extends beyond Osiris's death. His wife, Isis, is devastated and embarks on a dangerous quest to recover and restore him. Set's actions plunge the gods into conflict, disrupting the divine order. Isis's efforts to revive Osiris led to further strife, highlighting the widespread impact of Set's actions.

Long-Term Consequences

The story of Osiris, Isis, and Set demonstrates the long-term consequences of cunning manipulation. Set's actions lead to Osiris's death and create a ripple effect that disturbs both the divine and mortal worlds. The legacy of Set's deceitful actions reverberates through Egyptian Mythology, underscoring the destructive power of jealousy and covert treachery.

The story of Set's manipulation of Osiris in ancient Egyptian mythology illustrates how jealousy and cunning can lead to catastrophic outcomes. Set's deceitful plan to eliminate Osiris, executed through a seemingly benign invitation and a hidden trap, results in Osiris's death and widespread chaos among the gods. The tragic consequences of Set's actions emphasize the destructive power of covert manipulation and its far-reaching impact on family and the broader world.

The Story of Kamsa and Krishna
(Hinduism)

In Hindu mythology, the story of Kamsa's overt bullying and tyranny towards his sister Devaki and her family is a stark example of how fear and desperation can lead to ruthless and tragic outcomes. This narrative highlights the destructive impact of direct oppression driven by paranoia and the desire to maintain power.

Ruthless Oppression
Prophetic Fear

Kamsa, the tyrannical king of Mathura, becomes terrified after hearing a prophecy that the eighth child of his sister. Devaki will be his downfall. This prophecy, a powerful belief system in Hindu mythology, fuels Kamsa's paranoia and desperate need to cling to power. His actions, driven by this belief, are direct and brutal as he devises a plan to prevent the prophecy from coming true.

Imprisonment and Control

To thwart the prophecy, Kamsa takes drastic measures by imprisoning Devaki and her husband, Vasudeva, in a dark, oppressive dungeon. This act of imprisonment is both a physical and psychological assault, as Kamsa seeks to dominate and control them, ensuring that any potential threat to his rule is contained.

Systematic Infanticide:

Kamsa's brutality escalates as he systematically kills each of Devaki's newborn children. This ruthless act is his way of directly confronting and eliminating the prophesied danger, using his power to enforce his will and suppress any challenge to his authority.

Tragic Outcome

Years of Suffering and Fear: The prolonged imprisonment and the relentless killing of her children cause immense suffering for Devaki and Vasudeva. The psychological torment and helplessness they endure highlight the devastating impact of Kamsa's ruthless actions. The constant threat to their family and the oppressive environment amplifies their prolonged suffering.

Krishna's Escape and Kamsa's Defeat

Despite Kamsa's efforts, Krishna, the eighth child, miraculously escapes from the dungeon. As Krishna grows, he returns to Mathura, confronts Kamsa, and defeats him in a dramatic battle. Krishna's victory not only restores justice but also. However, the trauma experienced by Devaki and Vasudeva and the fear instilled in the people of Mathura underscores the tragic consequences of Kamsa's tyranny

Broader Implications

The story of Kamsa and Krishna illustrates how the king's fear-driven and oppressive actions lead to widespread suffering and turmoil. The tragic outcomes extend beyond the immediate family, affecting the entire kingdom and demonstrating the far-reaching consequences of direct tyranny and oppression.

Kamsa's story in Hindu mythology exemplifies how ruthless oppression, driven by paranoia and a desire for control, can result in tragic consequences. His direct actions—imprisoning Devaki, systematically killing her children, and ruling through fear—lead to years of suffering for his family and ultimately to his downfall. The narrative underscores how unchecked fear and power can cause profound harm, disrupting lives on both personal and societal levels.

The Story of Hades and Persephone
(Greek Mythology)

In Greek mythology, the tale of Hades and Persephone serves as a poignant example of how cunning manipulation and psychological control can lead to tragic outcomes. The relationship between Hades and Persephone are both familial and marital—Hades, the god of the Underworld, abducts Persephone, who is his niece, to make her his wife, resulting in a complex and powerful myth that explains the origin of the seasons.

The Abduction and Psychological Control

Abduction: Hades, the god of the Underworld, becomes infatuated with Persephone, the daughter of Demeter, the goddess of agriculture, and Zeus, making Persephone his niece. Driven by his desire, Hades devises a dramatic and cunning plan to abduct Persephone while she is picking flowers in a meadow. In an instant, he drags her down to his dark realm, separating her from the vibrant life of the Earth and her mother.

Psychological Manipulation

Once in the Underworld, Hades begins to exert psychological control over Persephone. He isolates her from the world above, severing her connection with

Demeter and the life she once knew. This isolation is a calculated strategy, designed to weaken Persephone's resistance and slowly manipulate her into accepting her new role as queen of the Underworld. By controlling her environment and cutting off her ties to the world she loves, Hades creates a sense of inevitability around her fate.

Assertion of Dominance

Hades employs subtle yet powerful tactics to assert his dominance over Persephone. He ensures that she has no means of escape and introduces a crucial element to bind her to the Underworld—pomegranate seeds. The pomegranate, rich in symbolic meaning, represents life, death, and binding contracts. By tricking Persephone into consuming food from the Underworld, Hades enforces a rule that ties her to his realm, ensuring that she must return for a portion of each year, even if she eventually leaves. The act of eating the pomegranate seeds not only signifies Persephone's binding to the Underworld but also symbolizes the duality of her existence between life and death, as well as the changing seasons.

Tragic Outcomes

Emotional Impact

Persephone's abduction and enforced isolation cause immense emotional turmoil, not just for her, but for her mother, Demeter. Demeter's grief at the loss of her daughter is so profound that it disrupts the natural order. Her mourning manifests as the barren, cold months of winter, when nothing grows on

Earth, symbolizing the widespread impact of Hades' manipulative actions.

Familial Disruption

The trauma inflicted on Persephone and Demeter extends beyond personal sorrow, leading to a disruption of the natural world. Demeter's prolonged grief results in famine and desolation, testing the bond between mother and daughter. The natural balance of the Earth is thrown into disarray, illustrating how Hades' cunning manipulation reverberates far beyond the Underworld, affecting both the divine and mortal realms.

Persephone's Compromise

The psychological toll of Persephone's role as the queen of the Underworld is a central theme. Her compromise, dividing her time between the Underworld and Earth, is a poignant reflection of the manipulative tactics of Hades. The power she gains is overshadowed by the circumstances of her abduction and the loss of her former life, a psychological burden that she carries.

Hades' cunning manipulation and psychological control during Persephone's abduction cause profound emotional and familial disruption. His methods of isolation and dominance not only affect Persephone but also her mother, Demeter, and the natural world. The pomegranate, symbolizing life, death, and binding contracts, highlights the depth of Persephone's struggle and the duality of her existence. This myth serves as a powerful illustration of the tragic outcomes of covert manipulation, showing how such actions deeply impact individuals, their relationships, and the world around them.

Reflections on Family Discord and Faminemies

Covert bullying within families has been a persistent issue across history, cultures, and religious contexts, characterized by manipulation and control. Its impact has shaped personal relationships and influenced broader social and political dynamics. By exploring its deep roots in various cultural and religious traditions, we gain insight into how these subtle behaviors have transcended time and space, affecting individuals and families alike.

The historical and religious examples serve as reminders of the long-lasting consequences of covert bullying within families. These stories illustrate the ways in which manipulation and family discord can lead to profound personal and societal outcomes, showing that the effects of covert bullying often reach far beyond the immediate family circle. These patterns of manipulation and control continue to resonate, revealing the complexities of human relationships across generations.

THE WANNABE BULLY

The wannabe bully isn't inherently malevolent but rather a nuanced individual within interpersonal dynamics, a propelled by a blend of insecurity, ambition, and a yearning for validation. This persona is often marked by a penchant for mirroring the conduct of more dominant figures, aiming to establish their presence within social hierarchies where power and influence are perceived. Yet, unlike the bully, who radiates confidence and authority, the wannabe bully lacks genuine self-assurance, depending on imitation and emulation to navigate social encounters.

It's important to recognize that many people in society can be classified as wannabe bullies. This large group plays a key role in the success of covert bullies, as they rely on the support and collaboration of these wannabe bullies to maintain their power and influence. The covert bully strategically uses these individuals, not through formal agreements, but through an implicit and hidden understanding that sustains their manipulative behavior.

The Wannabe Bully Personality

This type of wannabe bully is motivated by a profound sense of inadequacy and a desperate need for validation. Their low self-esteem makes them easy prey for stronger, more dominant personalities, whom they idolize and attempt to imitate. They align themselves with individuals they perceive as powerful or influential, adopting their behaviors, language, and attitudes in an effort to gain acceptance and approval. This mimicry is often more about gaining social standing than any real desire to bully others.

The insecure followers' actions are marked by inconsistency. Lacking genuine confidence, they struggle to convincingly assert themselves or maintain the authority they try to project. Their attempts to emulate more assertive individuals often come across as forced or contrived, further highlighting their insecurity. This creates a pattern where they oscillate between trying to fit in and fearing rejection.

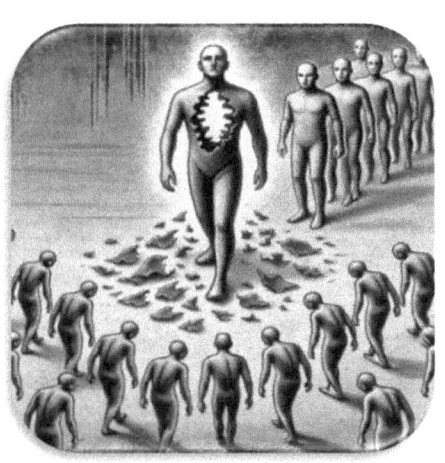

The Insecure Followers

In social dynamics, these individuals rarely take the lead in harmful behavior, but instead follow the example of more confident bullies. They may engage in subtle forms of manipulation, gossip, or exclusion, but only when they feel safe under the umbrella of a stronger personality. Their need to belong and fear of being targeted themselves keeps them tethered to the actions of others, making them complicit in the

bullying without the courage to act independently. Ultimately, the insecure follower's drive to mimic those in power stems from a fear of being seen as weak or insignificant. This lack of self-assurance not only affects their interactions with others but also reinforces a cycle of self-doubt, as they are constantly seeking validation through imitation rather than developing their own sense of identity.

The Opportunist

The opportunistic wannabe bully is driven by a relentless pursuit of self-promotion. Their defining trait is adaptability, which allows them to shift their behavior to align with whoever holds power. This constant adaptability reminds us to stay vigilant in our interactions. With little sense of personal ethics or loyalty, they base their decisions entirely on what will help them achieve their immediate objectives.

With their cunning nature, these individuals often flatter and mimic the dominant bully, presenting themselves as indispensable allies while secretly plotting their own rise. However, while lacking the skill of more calculated individuals like frenemies, their subtle manipulation is to be considered. As a result, they are more easily exposed. They stir up discord and reinforce the bully's actions, all to maintain favor within the dominant power structure.

In social settings, the opportunistic wannabe bully is known for their self-serving motivations. They spread gossip, form strategic alliances, and quietly sabotage others to stay in good standing with the bully. They maintain a façade of friendliness and cooperation, but their true motivations are purely self-serving. This should make us wary and guarded in our interactions with them.

Ultimately, the opportunistic wannabe bully's goal is personal gain—whether that means climbing the social ladder, securing career advantages, or gaining access to exclusive opportunities. Their relationships are transactional, based on what others can offer regarding status or influence. This opportunistic behavior sharply contrasts with the genuine connection and support that foster healthy, meaningful relationships, under-

scoring the negative impact of their actions.

The Impressionable Youth

In their vulnerability, they're naturally drawn to those who seem powerful or famous, especially bullies. From a young age, they instinctively seek someone to follow, gravitating toward individuals who display dominance, aggression, or rebellious behavior. While they may harbor similar negative tendencies, these impulses remain dormant, unable to emerge independently.

By aligning with a more dominant covert or overt bully, they find a sense of belonging and a way to channel their repressed hostility, gaining excitement and protection. This behavior reflects the societal influences around them, emphasizing the need for the entire community to step in, advocate for change, and offer positive role models.

Even though 'good kids' embody stability, kindness, and re-

sponsibility, they often fail to be popular and capture the attention of impressionable youth as much as the bold actions of a bully. To the vulnerable youth, bullying, mocking, and excluding another child can appear as a form of bravery. In their quest to be seen as bold, they mimic the bully's behavior, believing it will grant them the same power and acceptance. However, unlike bullies, these youth are more moldable. With proper awareness and guidance, they can easily be steered toward a positive path—if that path becomes popular, they will follow it without hesitation.

The Envious Underling

Driven by deep-seated feelings of inadequacy and bitterness, the envious individual fixates on those they perceive as more successful or accomplished. This fixation is a result of their own insecurities and a need to validate their self-worth. Unable to confront or undermine these individuals alone due to their own perceived inferiority, they wait for an opportunity to align themselves with someone more assertive. When they find a dominant figure willing to carry out acts of sabotage or manipulation, the envious individual quickly attaches themselves, using the situation to mask their insecurities.

They take satisfaction in seeing others brought down, but only through the safety of following in someone else's shadow. Their actions are often passive-aggressive, subtly contributing to the efforts to discredit or undermine others. By aligning with a more dominant personality, they can justify their behavior as part of a group dynamic, avoiding responsibility while achieving their vindictive goals. This toxic combination of jealousy and insecurity drives them to perpetuate harm, all while skillfully hiding behind the more overt actions of others, never fully exposing their true intentions.

The Wannabe Bully Characteristics

Mimicry

The wannabe bully often mimics the bully's language, gestures, and mannerisms to project confidence and authority. However, their imitation may come across as contrived or insincere, lacking the authenticity of genuine leadership.

Passive Aggression

Unable to assert themselves directly, the wannabe bully may resort to passive-aggressive tactics to express their frustrations or exert control over others. This can include subtle jabs, backhanded compliments, or underhanded schemes to undermine their perceived rivals.

Validation Seeking

Craving validation and approval from their peers and authority figures, the wannabe bully often seeks reassurance and affirmation of their worthiness within social circles. They may go to great lengths to curry favor with those they perceive as influential, using flattery or manipulation to gain acceptance.

Inconsistency

Despite their efforts to emulate the bully, the wannabe bully's behavior may lack consistency and conviction. They may vacillate between assertive and submissive roles, depending on the social context and the perceived reactions of others. This inconsistency can undermine their credibility and effectiveness as a bully.

Vulnerability to Manipulation

The wannabe bully is susceptible to manipulation by more dominant personalities, who may exploit their insecurities and desire for acceptance. They may be drawn into schemes or conflicts orchestrated by others, unwittingly becoming pawns in a more significant power play.

Animal Simulations of the Wannabe Bully

Mimic Octopus

The mimic octopus is renowned for its ability to imitate the appearance and behaviors of other sea creatures, such as lionfish, flatfish, and sea snakes. Similarly, the wannabe bully mimics the language, gestures, and mannerisms of more dominant figures to project confidence and authority.

Hyenas

Hyenas are known for their scavenging behavior, often relying on the kills made by more dominant predators such as lions. Like hyenas, the wannabe bully operates on the periphery of power, scavenging opportunities and validation from more dominant figures.

Vultures

Much like vultures that wait for the right moment to swoop in and exploit a weakened situation, wannabe bullies bide their time, waiting for moments of vulnerability created by the main covert bully. In these moments, they seize the opportunity to assert themselves, often relying on the misfortunes of others to boost their own status.

The mimic octopus, hyenas, and vultures serve as fitting metaphors for wannabe bullies. They illustrate their reliance on imitation, lack of genuine self-assurance, and the delicate balance they maintain in navigating social dynamics. Recognizing these comparisons offers more profound insights into the behaviors and motivations of wannabe bullies in human interactions.

The wannabe bully occupies a unique and often precarious position within social dynamics, torn between their aspirations for dominance and their underlying insecurities. While they may display behaviors similar to those of a true bully, their lack of genuine confidence and authority sets them apart, making them more vulnerable to manipulation and exploitation.

Understanding the complexities of the wannabe bully's personality and behavior can illuminate the intricate dynamics of social hierarchies and the complex interplay between power, influence, and insecurity in interpersonal relationships.

THE COVERT BULLY'S TARGET
(*THE HOST*)

The third part of the covert bully triad dynamic is the host—the target of the familial "vampire" Initially, these individuals may serve as the primary target of the clandestine bully, but over time, they often become scapegoats, absorbing blame, criticism, and emotional abuse from the entire family. This role can extend to others connected to the bully, as the bully ensures the target loses social respect through tactics such as spreading rumors and subtle gestures, making them easy prey for everyone to exploit.

It is crucial to understand that the target does not choose this role; it is imposed upon them by family members who seek to deflect attention from their flaws and maintain control over the family narrative. The targets of bullying are a diverse group, varying widely in demographics, personality traits, and social standing. Specific individuals may be more vulnerable to bullying based on perceived weaknesses, social isolation, or differences in identity. For example, children, due to their developmental stage, often carry this "target energy" into adolescence, continuing to face bullying. Similarly, individuals with disabilities or mental health challenges may face heightened risks due to social stigma and discrimination.

The goal of the covert bully is often to target someone seen as a threat to their success or position within the family. This target is usually viewed as a "competitor" who must be undermined. Depending on the context, victims can take on different roles within the family dynamic, such as "the Competitor," "the Close One," or "the Outsider."

> **The Competitor** is seen as a direct threat to the bully and is diminished to prevent them from succeeding. This often leads to feelings of jealousy and emotional rivalry.
>
> **The Close One** is exploited by being burdened with excessive responsibilities to meet the bully's emotional needs, leading to an imbalanced and unhealthy relationship that weakens their independence.
>
> **The Outsider** feels marginalized and excluded from family decisions, fostering loneliness and alienation.

The covert bully's target is often, but not always, a scapegoat—someone unfairly blamed for the group's problems. However, they can also be assigned other roles, such as the "black sheep," the "competitor," the "confidant," or the "outsider." Regardless of the role, these individuals are typically sensitive and vulnerable to emotional abuse. They often become outlets for the family's unresolved conflicts, leading to a relentless erosion of their self-esteem and mental health.

The dynamics that lead to someone becoming a scapegoat—a person unfairly blamed for the problems of others—are complex and multifaceted. Often, the scapegoat is chosen because they are different, more sensitive, unconfrontational or unwilling to conform to the family's toxic behaviors. Their presence challenges the status quo, making them an easy target for those seeking to project their insecurities and failings. The covert bully exploits the scapegoat's vulnerability, using them to bolster their sense of power and control.

Understanding these examples provides a broader context for the host's experience and highlights the pervasive nature of this destructive dynamic throughout human history. Ultimately, this knowledge empowers those unfairly targeted to reclaim their self-worth and break free from the cycle of abuse. In the following sections, we will delve into the characteristics of the host and explore notable examples of hosting and scapegoating in history and religion.

UNDERSTANDING THE CHARACTERISTICS OF THE TARGET

Understanding why some individuals are targeted by covert bullies involves considering the psychological and sociological factors that make them more vulnerable.

Perceived Weakness

Covert bullies often exploit perceived weaknesses as a primary tactic, targeting individuals they view as shy, introverted, or lacking in self-confidence. Those who exhibit signs of vulnerability become easy prey for manipulation, which can be psychologically draining, leaving the target feeling exhausted and depleted. This exploitation of perceived weakness is especially harmful because it undermines the target's ability to assert themselves and set boundaries, further entrenching their vulnerability. As a result, targets who struggle with self-assertion or boundary-setting become even more susceptible to these covert tactics, making it easier for bullies to manipulate and control them.

Recognizing and understanding this dynamic is crucial for empowering these individuals to acknowledge their strengths and protect themselves from further exploitation.

Lack of Boundaries

Family members who struggle to assert themselves or establish clear boundaries are prime targets for Faminemies. Their difficulty in saying no or standing up for themselves, often driven by a fear of being perceived as rude or disrespectful, creates an environment where bullies can easily encroach upon and manipulate their personal space without resistance. This lack of boundaries allows the bully to exert control and leaves the target feeling overwhelmed by the demands placed upon them.

As feelings of powerlessness and resentment escalate, it becomes increasingly crucial to grasp the significance of establishing and upholding firm boundaries. This action is vital in shielding oneself from manipulation and exploitation, while reclaiming personal power in the face of such challenges.

People Pleasers

People pleasers, known for their compassion and empathy, are often the targets of covert bullies within families and among relatives. These individuals, who go out of their way to help others, are vulnerable to manipulation by family members who exploit their desire to please. Despite their efforts, these gestures are often not reciprocated, leaving the people pleaser feeling unappreciated and taken for granted.

Covert bullies are like vampires; they can smell what they perceive as weakness and quickly identify people pleasers as their targets. They see the people pleasers' empathy and desire to please as traits they would never embody and thus consider their weaknesses. As a result, they know that the people pleaser is someone they can 'host on, draining their energy and self-worth.

The covert bully employs subtle tactics such as guilt-tripping, gaslighting, and passive-aggressive behavior to control and manipulate the people-pleaser, ensuring their own dominance and satisfaction while leaving the target increasingly drained and devalued. People-pleasers often find themselves taken advantage of or manipulated, leading to feelings of betrayal, disillusionment, and resentment. Their strong focus on pleasing others makes it difficult to establish healthy boundaries, resulting in an imbalance in family relationships where their needs are consistently overlooked or ignored.

Being a people pleaser can take a significant emotional toll. They may experience a complex web of emotional and psychological challenges, including low self-esteem, self-doubt, and anxiety. The constant need to please others and lift their spirits can also lead to burnout, as they neglect their needs and well-being.

By understanding how the desire to please others can be exploited within family dynamics, we can better support people-pleasers in setting healthy boundaries and protecting themselves from manipulation. It's crucial that we empower them to prioritize their own needs and well-being, not just as a solution, but as a vital step in fostering healthier family relationships.

Differences

In the intricate dynamics of family relationships, individuals who differ from the rest of the family can quickly become targets for siblings or other family members' bullying. These differences manifest in various ways, such as not physically resembling the rest of the family, having unconventional interests or hobbies, or expressing themselves in unique ways. Covert bullies within the family often view these differences as threats to their sense of normalcy or superiority, prompting them to target these individuals for ridicule, exclusion, or ostracism.

By recognizing these tactics and understanding the dynamics at play, individuals can begin to assert themselves and set boundaries, thereby protecting themselves from covert bullying. Such bullying often leaves targets feeling isolated, filled with self-doubt, and plagued by inadequacy as their family members marginalize them. The family unfairly targets these individuals because their differences challenge the status quo. The covert bullies exploit these differences to reinforce their control and dominance within the family, perpetuating a cycle of emotional abuse and manipulation. Understanding these dynamics is key to breaking free from this cycle and reclaiming personal power.

Overgiving

Excessive generosity can make individuals vulnerable to exploitation, especially covert bullies. Driven to please others or avoid conflict, these individuals become easy targets for manipulation that drains them energetically and financially. Covert bullies excel at identifying and exploiting people with a people-pleasing mindset, taking advantage of their kindness to manipulate them into doing their bidding or surrendering their resources. This exploitative dynamic, where covert bullies increasingly take more from these individuals as they become more generous, leaves them feeling used and breeds resentment, frustration, and betrayal. Recognizing this dynamic is crucial, as it can lead to financial and emotional depletion rooted in a misplaced sense of generosity. By resisting the urge to overextend and fostering self-awareness and assertiveness, these individuals can protect themselves from further exploitation while maintaining genuine generosity without falling target to covert bullying.

The Self-Blamer: Targets frequently internalize blame, believing
they are at fault for the bullying.
This self-blame can further damage their self-esteem and make it
harder for them to recognize and

address the abuse. The self-blamer often grows up in an envi-
ronment where others constantly compare them to a favored
sibling or family member. This comparison creates a deep-
seated belief that they are inherently flawed or inadequate.
The lack of recognition and validation from a parent can make
the unfavored child feel responsible for the adverse treatment
they receive, leading to a cycle of self-blame and self-doubt.

In adulthood, this internalized blame manifests in various detri-
mental ways. The self-blamer tends to constantly question
their worth and abilities, attributing any form of mistreatment to
their own perceived shortcomings. This mindset can cause
them to endure toxic relationships, whether personal or professional. In the workplace, for instance, they might tolerate a
boss's abusive behavior, believing they deserve it or can
somehow fix the situation by improving themselves.

In romantic relationships, the self-blamer might tolerate abusive or manipulative behavior, rationalizing that they are the
problem and need to change. They may excessively apologize
and go to great lengths to avoid conflict, fearing that any disa-
greement or mistake will confirm their unworthiness, which can

lead to an imbalance of power in the relationship, with the self-blamer often ending up in a subordinate and emotionally draining position, where their needs and feelings are consistently overlooked or dismissed.

The tendency to internalize blame also impacts the self-blamer's ability to seek help. It takes immense courage to admit being bullied or mistreated, and it's important to remember that doing so does not expose any flaws. This isolation reinforces their belief that they are alone in their struggles and undeserving of support or empathy. However, it's crucial to remember that seeking help is a sign of strength, not weakness. It's a brave step towards healing and reclaiming your life. Breaking free from the cycle of self-blame is a journey that requires a conscious effort to reframe one's self-perception. It involves recognizing that the bullying and favoritism they've experienced were not their fault and that they have intrinsic worth and value.

Therapy, support groups, and building healthy relationships role in this process, offering a beacon of hope and a path toward healing. They provide a safe space for the self-blamers to share their experiences, gain insights, and receive support, helping them develop a more balanced and compassionate view of themselves. By addressing these deep-rooted issues, the self-blamer can gradually rebuild their self-esteem and learn to set boundaries, fostering healthier interactions and a more fulfilling life.

The non-confrontational

Non-confrontational family members often become prime targets for covert bullying because they tend to avoid conflict, making it difficult for them to stand up to the bully. The bully often misinterprets their passive nature as agreement or acceptance, which only emboldens them.

Covert bullying within families usually begins subtly, making it challenging for non-confrontational individuals to recognize and confront it. Behaviors such as backhanded compliments, subtle disrespect, exclusion from family activities, spreading rumors, or undermining the target's confidence can lead to self-doubt and fear of being wrong. This fear can paralyze them, preventing them from speaking out or defending themselves.

Although these targets deeply feel the injustice of their treatment, their fear of conflict and desire to avoid creating tension often override their inner discomfort. They may worry about being perceived as overly sensitive or overreacting, leading them to downplay their experiences. Growing up in an environment of favoritism can further erode their confidence, causing them to doubt their worth and believe their concerns are invalid. This lack of self-assurance reinforces their passivity and makes them feel that standing up for themselves is futile or harmful.

When covert bullying begins within the family, non-confrontational targets might resort to avoidance or appeasement as coping mechanisms. Unfortunately, other family members often misinterpret this behavior as acceptance, leading wannabe bullies to join in targeting the target. As a result, these individuals may isolate themselves further, avoiding family gatherings or interactions, deepening their vulnerability and helplessness. They might avoid seeking help, fearing not being believed or that it could lead to further retargetization, which deepens their reluctance to address the issue directly.

Over time, the pressure of enduring covert bullying without confronting it can cause suppressed anger, frustration, and hurt to build up inside the target which can eventually reach a breaking point, resulting in an explosive outburst that may be dramatic and intense, potentially involving violent behavior or an emotional breakdown. Unfortunately, this reaction can make the target appear unstable or "crazy" to other family members, providing the bully with further ammunition to discredit them.

This cycle is particularly damaging, as the target's outburst often appears out of the blue. Instead of recognizing the long-term abuse that led to the eruption, family members may only see the dramatic reaction and side with the bully, who now has an opportunity to paint the target as irrational and volatile. This misinterpretation reinforces the target's isolation and further damages their self-esteem.

Breaking free from this cycle requires developing assertiveness and self-advocacy skills which involves learning to recognize and validate their experiences and feelings, understanding that their discomfort and pain are legitimate, and building the confidence to stand up for themselves. Support from therapy, assertiveness training, and encouraging relationships can help targets regain control and empower themselves.

By gradually learning to confront covert bullying behavior and seeking help when needed, non-confrontational targets can reclaim their power and begin to set healthy boundaries. This empowerment process can lead to more respectful and balanced interactions within the family, fostering a sense of safety and self-worth.

The Self-Gaslighter

The self-gaslighter is a product of prolonged exposure to covert bullying and gaslighting. Covert bullying can be manifested as subtle insults, exclusion, or undermining of one's abilities, while gaslighting involves the manipulation of someone's perception of reality. Over time, these forms of constant psychological manipulation cause individuals to doubt their thoughts, feelings, and perceptions.

This characteristic emerges when the person, feeling isolated and disbelieved, loses confidence in their internal judgment. As a survival mechanism, they start questioning their own reality, effectively gaslighting themselves. This tendency often develops after a covert bully consistently invalidates or subtly manipulates a self-gaslighter. The result is deep internal conflict and a weakened sense of discernment, leaving the self-gaslighter vulnerable to further manipulation. With diminished trust in their own instincts, they become increasingly reliant on the bully's version of reality. This cycle of self-doubt and confusion allows the covert abuse to persist, keeping the self-gaslighter trapped in a state of uncertainty. Understanding the role of the covert bullying process can help individuals feel validated and understood in their experiences.

Social Standing within Families and Relatives

Covert bullies among relatives often target individuals based on their social standing or perceived lack of a solid social standing, particularly high-potential individuals who are vulnerable due to their position within the family.

These bullies aim to undermine self-worth and exploit feelings of inferiority through subtle tactics, making it difficult for targets to confront or denounce the behavior. For example, bullies may make snide remarks about the target's social circle or belittle their achievements, maintaining power and control through these underhanded actions.

Targets of covert bullying often face a myriad of psychological challenges. They feel marginalized, excluded, and rejected within their families, leading to deep loneliness and isolation. This emotional pain creates complex psychological challenges, eroding self-esteem and affecting various areas of life, such as academic performance, social interactions, and mental health. Many targets internalize the negative messages they receive, leading to feelings of shame and inadequacy. This, in turn, creates a cycle of self-doubt and self-criticism, making it difficult for them to recognize and celebrate their own strengths.

The long-term effects can be profound, influencing the target's relationships, career choices, and sense of self-worth well into adulthood. Recognizing the covert nature of this bullying—especially against high-potential individuals perceived as socially inferior—is the first step towards addressing it.

Birth Order and Targetization in Families

Understanding the role of birth order is crucial in determining which family members become targets of covert bullying. The dynamics associated with being the oldest, middle, youngest, or only child can significantly influence how siblings interact with each other and how they are treated within the family. This understanding empowers us to shed light on why specific individuals are more susceptible to becoming targets of covert bullying.

Oldest Child

Parents often view the eldest child as the family pioneer, a role that comes with greater re-sponsibilities and higher expec-tations. As the firstborn, the eld-est child may face significant pressure to meet these de-

mands. However, their sensitivity or shyness can make them vulnerable to covert bullying from older relatives or peers of the same age.

Such hidden manipulation or emotional abuse often goes un-noticed by parents, who may lack the necessary experience in parenting to recognize these signs. Additionally, with the birth of more siblings, the eldest child may also face criticism from younger siblings, further exposing them to bullying.

This combination of pressures makes the eldest child suscepti-ble to bullying from multiple family members. At the same time, parents, despite their good intentions, may remain unaware of the deeper issues occurring due to their lack of experience.

The Middle Child

The middle child often struggles to find their place within the fam-ily dynamic. They often feel ne-glected or overlooked because they aren't the pioneering oldest or the adored youngest. Covert bullies may exploit these feelings, targeting the middle child for manipulation and emotional abuse. In response, the middle child might develop an overly people-pleasing nature as a protection mechanism. Addition-ally, they may become scapegoats, unfairly blamed for family issues to deflect attention from the real problems, further erod-ing bullies may exploit these feelings, targeting the middle child for manipulation and emotional abuse. In response, the middle child might develop an overly people-pleasing nature as a protection mechanism. Additionally, they may become a scapegoat, unfairly blamed for family issues to deflect atten-tion from the real problems, further eroding their self-esteem and leaving long-lasting emotional scars.

The Youngest Child

The youngest child, often seen as the family's " baby, " may receive much attention and affection. However, they are also vulnerable to covert bullying from the older siblings or just the one above them in age. Feeling

threatened by the attention the youngest receives, this sibling may act out of jealousy or a desire to assert dominance. They might undermine the youngest child's confidence, perceiving them as less capable or mature. Over time, this childhood jealousy can develop into a lifelong mission to sabotage the youngest child's success.

The Only Child

Only children may not have siblings to compete with, but they can still become targets of covert bullying from other relatives or extended family members. The love and attention they receive from their parents can create a strong foundation for success, but this potential can also ignite jealousy in other parents with children of the same age. In response, these relatives might go to great lengths to undermine the only child, covertly working to ensure their children outshine them. This jealousy can turn the entire extended family into covert bullies, all working subtly to sabotage the only child's success.

The Overlooked

Children who are not favored by parents often become targets of familial bullying. Favoritism can arise from various reasons, such as physical resemblance to the parent, perceived attractiveness, or characteristics that a parent admires. This disparity in attention affects the unfavored child deeply. They may develop psychological issues due to perceived inadequacy and a constant need for parental approval. Such children are vulnerable to bullying within the family, which can extend into social settings like school or work and later into romantic relationships.

Birth Order and Familial Favoritism
Unpacking Targetization Dynamics

Understanding the impact of birth order is crucial for recognizing patterns of covert bullying within families. Each sibling's position brings unique challenges and vulnerabilities that covert bullies might exploit. For instance:

> **Oldest Child:** Faces high expectations and potential resentment.

> **Middle Child:** May struggle with feelings of neglect and invisibility.

Youngest Child: Often perceived as more manipulable, potentially bullied by older siblings.

Only Child: Could be overwhelmed by intense parental focus or scrutiny.

Overlooked Child: Suffers from lack of parental favoritism, leading to feelings of inadequacy and vulnerability to bullying from both family and social circles.

Identifying these dynamics not only sheds light on the problem but also opens the door for positive change. It motivates families to foster healthier relationships and protect all members from emotional abuse, effectively addressing and preventing covert bullying.

Long-Term Effects

The deep-seated sense of inadequacy from not being favored can lead to ongoing retargetization and a lack of self-respect across various stages of life. This is often evident in romantic relationships, where the unfavored child, seeking constant validation, may develop an unhealthy fear of rejection. As a result, they might tolerate toxic dynamics, mistaking them for normalcy. These individuals are often drawn to partners who exhibit controlling or abusive behaviors, a reflection of unresolved issues rooted in their childhood experiences. This cycle of dysfunctional relationships and emotional turmoil, rooted in familial dynamics, underscores the lasting effects of not being the favored child. It highlights the urgency and significance of addressing these issues, as it is essential for breaking the cycle of retargetization and fostering emotional resilience.

The Jocker

The target who assumes the role of the "joker" in a family dynamic often develops their people-pleasing tendencies such as a survival mechanism in response to covert bullying and emotional manipulation.

They may sense tension or conflict within the family from a young age, particularly when they are made the scapegoat or the object of ridicule. To deflect attention from their pain and avoid further bullying, they adopt humor and light-heartedness as a way to gain approval and acceptance from others.

Their need to please others and keep the peace often overshadows their sense of self-worth as they learn that earning approval through entertainment or minimizing conflict is more valuable than asserting their own needs. Although this people-pleasing behavior provides temporary relief from criticism, it becomes a deeply ingrained pattern that sacrifices their self-respect.

They prioritize harmony in the family over standing up for themselves, fearing that challenging the dynamics may lead to more isolation or emotional harm. As the "joker," they learn to suppress their emotions, using humor to mask more profound feelings of insecurity and pain. Over time, this role becomes both a shield and a prison as they struggle to break free from the expectations placed on them by family members while their self-worth continues to erode beneath the surface. The more they conform to this role, the harder it becomes for them to recognize and prioritize their own emotional needs, leaving them vulnerable to further manipulation and emotional neglect.

THE SCAPEGOAT

Scapegoating is an ingrained aspect of human behavior, often rooted in familial dynamics and human nature. Historically, it has emerged from differences between siblings, where one— usually inclined towards manipulation and subtle bullying—becomes the "vampire" (covert bully). In contrast, the other, more sensitive sibling becomes the scapegoat. This dynamic reflects a recurring pattern in human relationships, illustrating how deeply embedded these behaviors are in our psyche.

Although the term "scapegoat" comes from the Hebrew Bible, the practice of shifting blame or guilt onto another entity appears in numerous cultures and traditions:

The Evolution and Origin of Scapegoating

Scapegoating has been a deeply rooted psychological phenomenon in societies for centuries. Internal and external forms of scapegoating have had significant consequences, often justified through religious practices and viewed as part of divine reasoning. The term "scapegoat" originates from a Hebrew Bible ritual, highlighting the enduring role scapegoating has played in shaping how societies distribute blame and assign responsibility.

The Day of Atonement (Yom Kippur)

The concept of a "scapegoat" originates from an ancient Jewish ritual described in the Book of Leviticus (Leviticus 16:8-10). During Yom Kippur, the Day of Atonement, they chose two goats for a sacred ceremony. One was sacrificed as a sin offering, while the other, known as the "scapegoat," was symbolically loaded with the sins of the people. The High Priest would place his hands on the scapegoat, transferring the sins of the Israelites onto it. This goat, now burdened with the sins, was then sent into the wilderness, symbolizing the removal of the community's transgressions.

Christian Tradition

The concept of the scapegoat" in Christianity is intricately linked to the idea of redemption and salvation through sacrifice. In Christian tradition, Jesus Christ is revered as the ultimate "scapegoat," believed to have shouldered the sins of humanity through his crucifixion and death. This represents a profound sacrifice that embodies divine love and forgiveness, a testament to the compassion and grace of the Christian faith. Christians view this act ofsacrifice as offering salvation to humankind and relieving them of the burden of sin, a feat that inspires awe and reverence.

In contrast, the Islamic faith adopts a different perspective. According to Islamic teachings, Jesus was not crucified; instead, God raised him up to heaven. In Islam, God is merciful and would not allow an innocent person to be killed unjustly for the sins of others. Each individual is seen as responsible for their actions, and forgiveness is attained through repentance and direct divine mercy. This fosters a profound sense of connection, as each person has a direct relationship with God, without the need for a sacrificial atonement.

These two perspectives reflect a multifaceted understanding of sacrifice and atonement. The concept of the scapegoat plays a pivotal role in shaping the theological beliefs of both Christianity and Islam. The differences in their interpretations are significant. Christian theology emphasizes redemption through symbolic sacrifice, while Islam highlights individual justice and a direct relationship with God through repentance.

Leviticus 16:8-10

God instructs Aaron to cast lots for the two goats—one for the Lord and the other for the scapegoat. Aaron is to offer the goat chosen for the Lord as a sin sacrifice. The other goat, designated as the scapegoat, is to be

kept alive, presented before the Lord and then sent into the wilderness to make atonement as the scapegoat.

Ancient Greece

In Ancient Greece, the concept of a "pharmakos" was similar. During times of crisis, such as famine or plague, a person (often a criminal or marginalized individual) would be chosen to bear the community's sins and misfortunes and be expelled or sacrificed.

Ancient Mesopotamia

Rituals involving the transfer of guilt and the expulsion of evil spirits were also present in ancient Mesopotamian cultures. These practices often involved symbolic acts to cleanse the community and appease the gods.

These rituals served both a symbolic and practical purpose, providing a tangible way for the community to atone for their sins and start anew. Transferring sins or guilt onto another entity became a powerful metaphor for dealing with collective responsibility and guilt.

THE STORY OF
SARAH, ABRAHAM, ISAAC, AND
ISHMAEL

People often tell the ancient narrative of Abraham, Sarah, Isaac, and Ishmael as a story of faith and divine promise. However, beneath the surface, it reveals a darker tale of covert bullying, indirect murder, and the ruthless pursuit of wealth and power. Sarah's actions demonstrate how her quiet manipulation and resolve to secure her son's inheritance triggered a sequence of events that deeply affected the lives of those involved and had a lasting influence on history.

Sarah

The Wife of Abraham

Sarah, initially named Sarai, was the wife of Abraham (originally Abram) and is a central figure in biblical and Torah narratives. Sarah, renowned for her beauty and devotion to Abraham, struggled profoundly with her inability to bear children—a source of profound sorrow in a culture that closely tied a woman's worth to her ability to produce heirs.

The weight of Sarah's barrenness was a heavy burden, especially because God had promised Abraham that he would be the father of a great nation. As the years passed and Sarah remained childless, her anxiety about fulfilling the divine promise grew. In the depths of her emotional turmoil, she made a desperate decision: she gave her maidservant, Hagar, to Abraham as a concubine in hopes of securing an heir.

Hagar

Hagar was an Egyptian servant in Sarah's household. The Torah and Bible do not extensively detail her origins, but she likely entered Sarah's service during Abraham and Sarah's time in Egypt.

It was not unusual in the ancient world when Sarah offered Hagar to Abraham. It was common for barren wives to provide their maidservants to their husbands as concubines, hoping the children born from this union would be considered legitimate heirs. Hagar, therefore, became pregnant with Abraham's child, Ishmael, Abraham's firstborn son.

The Strain Between Sarah and Hagar

The dynamics between Sarah and Hagar became strained after Hagar conceived. According to the Torah and Bible, once Hagar knew she was pregnant, she began to look down on Sarah, perhaps feeling superior because she could do what Sarah could not—bear a child for Abraham. This shift in attitude deeply wounded Sarah, who felt humiliated. In response to Hagar's perceived disrespect, Sarah treated her harshly, exerting her authority as the household's mistress.

The Torah and Bible state that Sarah dealt so harshly with Hagar that the pregnant servant fled into the wilderness. However, an angel of the Lord appeared to Hagar, instructing her to return to Sarah and submit to her, promising that her descendants through Ishmael would be too numerous to count. Hagar returned and gave birth to Ishmael. Despite the tension, Ishmael was raised in Abraham's household and was considered Abraham's heir for a time.

Sarah's Miraculous Conception

Years later, when Abraham and Sarah were very old, God renewed His promise to them, declaring that Sarah would bear a son, which seemed impossible to Sarah, who laughed at the idea, given her advanced age. Nevertheless, as the Lord had promised, Sarah conceived and gave birth to Isaac.

The birth of Isaac, while a joyous occasion, reignited Sarah's fears and insecurities. Now that she had her son, Sarah became increasingly protective of Isaac's future. This fear and insecurity, coupled with her experiences with Hagar, led Sarah to see Ishmael, about 13 years older than Isaac, as a threat to her son's inheritance. This perception of Ishmael as a threat would ultimately lead to the climax of their struggles.

The Climax of Their Struggles

The tension between Sarah and Hagar peaked when Sarah saw Ishmael either "mocking" or "playing" with Isaac. This incident may have been a ploy by Sarah to persuade Abraham to send Hagar and Ishmael away, ensuring that Ishmael would not share in Isaac's inheritance.

This situation greatly distressed Abraham, but God reassured him with two gracious promises. First, God promised Abraham that He would care for Ishmael and bless him, granting him a prosperous future and making him the father of a great nation. This divine reassurance, a beacon of God's compassion and mercy for both sons, is a powerful demonstration of God's wisdom that surpasses all human schemes. Through this story, faith in God's guidance over human affairs and his ultimate purpose shines through, even when events lead to tension and division.

Ishmael's Exile: Biblical and Torah Perspective

Islamic Perspective:

Ishmael's Exile and the Discovery of Zamzam:

Age:

Islamic Tradition: In Islamic tradition, Ishmael (Isma'il) was an infant while he was with his mother, Hagar. When Abraham (Ibrahim) left them in the barren valley near Mecca, Ishmael was still a baby.

Event Details: According to Islamic tradition, Hagar ran between the hills of Safa and Marwah after being left in the desert, desperately searching for water as Ishmael cried in distress. In response to Hagar's pleas, God sent the angel

Gabriel (Jibril), who miraculously caused water to spring forth from the ground where Ishmael lay, kicking his feet. This water source became the Zamzam well, a crucial element in Islamic pilgrimage rituals.

Biblical and Torah Perspective

In the Bible and Torah, Ishmael was approximately 16-17 years old when Abraham sent him and his mother, Hagar, away. The estimation comes from Ishmael being 13 years old when Isaac was born, and the exile occurred a few years later when Isaac was weaned.

Event Details: In this version, Sarah's fear that Ishmael, as the older son, would jeopardize Isaac's inheritance drove the exile. Ishmael was old enough to understand the gravity of the situation, and the Bible recounts how God provided for them by showing Hagar a well in the desert when they were on the brink of death.

The Sacrifice
Islamic Perspective
Age:

Islamic Tradition: In Islamic tradition, the event of Ishmael's near sacrifice occurs when Ishmael is older, likely a young

teenager or young adult. Although the exact age is not specified, he was old enough to have a mature conversation with his father, Abraham, about the significance of the vision Abraham received from God.

Event Details: In Islamic tradition, God tested Abraham's faith by commanding him to sacrifice his son, Ishmael. Both Abraham and Ishmael willingly submitted to God's will. However, at the last moment, God intervened and provided a ram to be sacrificed instead. This event is commemorated during Eid al-Adha, symbolizing submission to God's will and mercy.

Sacrifice: Biblical and Torah Perspective

Age:

Biblical and Torah Tradition: In the Bible and Torah, it is Isaac, not Ishmael, who is involved in the story of the near-sacrifice. Isaac was likely a young boy during this event, though his age is not detailed.

Event Details: In this narrative, God tests Abraham by asking him to sacrifice Isaac, his promised son. Just as Abraham is about to carry out the sacrifice, an angel intervenes, and a ram is provided as a substitute offering. This event underscores Isaac's role as the child of promise through whom God's covenant with Abraham would be fulfilled.

Summary of Ages in Relation to Key Events

Exile (Islamic Perspective): Ishmael is an infant.

Exile (Biblical and Torah Perspective): Ishmael is approximately 16-17 years old.

Discovery of Zamzam (Islamic Perspective): Ishmael is an infant.

The Sacrifice (Islamic Perspective): Ishmael is a young teenager or young adult.

The Sacrifice (Biblical and Torah Perspective): Isaac, not Ishmael, is the child involved, likely a young boy.

Manipulation, Inheritance, and Divine Will
Perspectives on Isaac and Ishmael

Biblical and Torah Perspective

In the Biblical and Torah narratives, Sarah's actions play a pivotal role in the complex dynamics of the family. Her determination to secure Isaac's inheritance and position as the chosen heir is evident in her insistence on exiling Hagar and Ishmael, mainly when Ishmael was a teenager. This can be interpreted as driven by jealousy and fear, as Ishmael, Abraham's firstborn, was old enough to understand inheritance dynamics and could potentially threaten Isaac. The narrative justifies Sarah's actions as necessary to protect the covenant through Isaac, portraying Ishmael as older and capable of challenging Isaac.

The timing of Ishmael's exile suggests a calculated move by Sarah to remove competition for Isaac's inheritance. This act can be seen as a form of manipulation, with Sarah influencing Abraham to prioritize Isaac. Similarly, Isaac's near-sacrifice emphasizes his role in the divine plan, presenting him as the true heir while subtly minimizing Ishmael's significance. By centering these pivotal events on Isaac, the narratives reinforce his legitimacy and marginalize Ishmael's place in the family.

At the heart of Sarah's actions is the pursuit of wealth, power, and legacy. Isaac's inheritance symbolized material wealth and the continuation of the divine promise and control over the family's future. Her decisions reflect the complexities of human ambition and familial dynamics, illustrating how far she was willing to go to protect her son's future.

Islamic Perspective

The Islamic narrative presents a different portrayal, focusing on divine providence and the faith of the key figures rather than human manipulation. Ishmael is depicted as an infant during the exile and later as a willing participant in the near-sacrifice. This portrayal avoids any implication of cunning or manipulation by Sarah or Abraham, emphasizing submission to God and the purity of faith instead.

In the Islamic tradition, the near-sacrifice highlights Ishmael's willingness to submit to divine will, a central theme in Islamic teachings. His role as the sacrificial son elevates his status, ensuring his importance in the lineage of prophets. The narrative positions Ishmael as a significant figure from the beginning, countering the dominant Biblical and Torah focus on Isaac. The Islamic account highlights Ishmael's significance and the divine protection he received, showcasing his resilience in overcoming hardships. It also illustrates that human attempts to control outcomes are ultimately powerless against the greater plan of divine will.

The stories of Isaac and Ishmael reveal profound themes of manipulation, inheritance, faith, and divine intervention. The Biblical and Torah perspectives emphasize Sarah's role in safeguarding Isaac's future through calculated actions, while the Islamic tradition highlights Ishmael's faith and submission to divine will, avoiding implications of human manipulation. These narratives, rich with the themes of faith and divine will, provide unique insights into the interplay between human decisions and divine plans, shaping the destinies of both Isaac and Ishmael.

The Interplay of Human Decisions and Divine Will
Lessons from Sarah, Hagar, and Their Sons

The story of Sarah, Hagar, Isaac, and Ishmael is a profound exploration of the psychological, moral, and spiritual dimensions of human behavior. Sarah's actions in securing Isaac's position as heir reveal the complexities of human decisions within a divine plan. Her choices, while ensuring her son's future, also reflect the moral dilemmas and emotional struggles inherent in fulfilling what she believed to be a divine promise. In this context, her fears and desires drove her to extreme measures against Hagar and Ishmael, illustrating the darker aspects of human behavior—covert manipulation, psychological bullying, and the relentless pursuit of control.

Abraham, caught in the tension between his love for Ishmael and his loyalty to Sarah and the divine promises, faced deep internal conflict. His decision to exile his firstborn son is a classic example of cognitive dissonance, where conflicting beliefs and values create profound psychological discomfort. This inner turmoil speaks to the enduring struggle of reconciling personal relationships with faith and duty.

For Ishmael, the experience of being cast out and nearly losing his life left indelible marks. Yet, his survival and the divine promise that he would become the father of a great nation underscore the resilience bestowed by faith and the mercy of divine will. Hagar, though initially a servant, emerged as the mother of a nation and a symbol of endurance and divine favor.

This narrative serves as a cautionary tale about the psychological and moral costs of manipulation, the pursuit of wealth, and the desire for dominance. It highlights the lengths to which individuals may go to protect what they value most, even at the expense of others. Yet, it also emphasizes the ultimate limitations of human schemes in the face of divine will. Despite Sarah's efforts, Ishmael's survival and eventual prosperity testify to the idea that destiny is ultimately shaped by forces beyond human control.

Through the interplay of human decisions and divine guidance, this story offers enduring lessons about faith, resilience, and the moral responsibilities that come with power and ambition.

Psychological and Sociological Perspectives

From a psychological and sociological perspective, scapegoating serves several critical functions within a group or community. By projecting blame onto a single individual or group, the majority can collectively relieve tension and avoid confronting their own shortcomings. This act of targeting a scapegoat paradoxically strengthens social bonds within the majority as they unite against a common "target." Moreover, scapegoating plays a crucial role in reinforcing the stability of social order and hierarchy, often marginalizing those who are different or perceived as weaker.

The "Vampire" (Covert Bully):

Nature: The "vampire" sibling naturally exhibits traits of covert bullying—manipulation, and psychological torment. This sibling often garners favor from parents and authority figures through charm, strategic behavior, and alignment with the family's expectations and values.

Behavior: This sibling subtly undermines the siblings, engaging in behaviors that isolate, criticize, and devalue the scapegoat sibling.

The "vampire" ensures their elevated status by keeping the target in a state of vulnerability and psychological distress.

The Scapegoat

Nature: In contrast to the "vampire," the scapegoat sibling is often sensitive, non-confrontational, and emotionally reactive. These traits make them more susceptible to the "vampire's" covert tactics.

Psychological Impact: Over time, the scapegoat sibling develops significant psychological issues—low self-esteem, anxiety, depression, and a pervasive sense of inadequacy. This emotional damage makes them increasingly undesirable in the eyes of the family and broader social circles.

The Scapegoating Process

Initial Favoritism: The family begins to show clear favoritism towards the "vampire" sibling, who aligns more closely with the family's ideals or appearance. This favored sibling receives more attention, praise, and resources, while the scapegoat sibling is subtly excluded and criticized.

Manipulation and Isolation: The "vampire" sibling uses covert tactics to manipulate family dynamics, ensuring the scapegoat sibling remains isolated and undervalued. The "vampire," tasting the power of favoritism, spreads rumors, highlights the scapegoat's weaknesses, and positions themselves as the superior sibling.

Psychological Breakdown: Constant exposure to covert bullying leads the scapegoat sibling to a psychological breakdown. They become increasingly anxious, depressed, and socially withdrawn, reinforcing the negative perceptions held by the family and others.

Labeling and Exclusion: As the scapegoat sibling's psychological state deteriorates, they are labeled as the problem within the family, often becoming truly problematic due to pressure and exclusion. This labeling absolves the family, particularly the "vampire" sibling, of responsibility for the dysfunction, casting all blame onto the scapegoat.

Ultimate Victory of the "Vampire":

The "vampire" sibling ultimately secures their favored position, cementing the scapegoat sibling's role as the family outcast. The cycle of favoritism and bullying is complete, with the scapegoat's undesirable status reinforcing the "vampire's" elevated position.

THE COMPLEXITY AND IMPACT OF UNCONSCIOUS IDEALISM

Unconscious idealism often begins in childhood and is shaped by early experiences of injustice, favoritism, or emotional neglect. These formative experiences create deeply ingrained beliefs and expectations about how the world should function, providing a sense of hope and purpose. These ideals guide actions, decisions, and emotional responses, serving as an internal compass for how life and relationships should unfold. However, when these ideals operate unconsciously, they can create significant vulnerabilities that affect individuals throughout their lives. Unconsciously, they can create significant vulnerabilities that affect individuals throughout their lives.

As people mature, unconscious idealism can manifest in various ways. For instance, it can lead to unrealistic expectations in relationships or careers, causing emotional stress and potential conflict. Idealists may overlook or deny the more complex and darker aspects of human nature, such as familial jealousy, emotional manipulation, covert competition, and toxic relationships. This idealistic lens often leads individuals to view the world as they wish it to be rather than as it truly is.

The disconnect between their idealism and reality leaves them vulnerable to exploitation and disappointment, as they may fail to recognize the true intentions of others. Over time, this pattern of idealism may result in repeated experiences of betrayal and emotional harm.

Individuals driven by unconscious idealism often feel persistently unlucky, as though cursed by bad luck, because their ideals prevent them from seeing the realities of the world. They may cling to a utopian vision, making them appear out of touch with reality and naive to others. This lifelong pattern can create a cycle of exploitation, where their idealism makes them easy targets for those who seek to manipulate or take advantage of their goodwill. However, these vulnerabilities hold the potential for profound growth.

By bringing unconscious ideals to light and reconciling them with the complexities of real life, individuals can transform their vulnerabilities into strengths. This process involves acknowledging the darker aspects of human nature and understanding how these aspects can coexist with positive traits like hope and optimism. It's about learning to be hopeful while being realistic about the potential for betrayal or disappointment. This balanced approach allows individuals to navigate the world more resiliently, authentically, and wisely.

Addressing unconscious idealism is not about abandoning one's ideals but balancing them with practical realities. Through awareness, self-compassion, and education, unconscious idealists can break free from the cycle of unrealistic expectations and emotional stress. This balanced approach, especially with self-compassion support, protects them from harm while maintaining their core values of kindness, compassion, and integrity. By confronting the trauma and beliefs that fuel unconscious idealism, individuals can foster emotional maturity, build healthier relationships, and lead more empowered, fulfilling lives.

Early Childhood Experiences

Family Influence

Early childhood experiences, particularly within the family environment, deeply embed the roots of unconscious idealism. Children absorb the values, beliefs, and behaviors of their parents and caregivers model. If a child grows up in a family that emphasizes harmony, kindness, and the inherent goodness of people, they are likely to adopt these ideals. However, without a balanced understanding of human complexities like jealousy, deceit, and unhealthy competition, the child may develop an unrealistic view of the world, setting the stage for future difficulties in recognizing and responding to toxic behaviors.

Childhood Injustice

Children who experience favoritism, injustice, or neglect may carry deep emotional wounds from the unequal treatment they endure. Witnessing or enduring such injustices can foster a longing for fairness, equality, and justice—ideals that the individual clings to in order to cope with the pain and trauma they have suffered. When these ideals remain unconscious, they can manifest as rigid, unrealistic expectations that perpetuate a cycle of disappointment and frustration. This cycle can sometimes trickle down to future generations, creating what can be seen as a 'generational curse'.

Parental Expectations

Parents often project their ideals onto their children, sometimes consciously but often unconsciously. For example, parents who value perfectionism or idealize family unity may instill these beliefs in their children. A child who internalizes these expectations may grow up constantly striving to meet them, believing they must always be perfect or prioritize family above all else, even at their own expense. This mindset fosters unconscious idealism, where the child's beliefs about themselves and others are heavily influenced by these early teachings, often to the detriment of their well-being.

Children of Idealistic Parents

Children raised by idealistic parents may develop an unrealistic view of their family and the world. These parents, driven by their ideals, may overlook or deny malice within family members, believing that all family members inherently share the exact nature. However, human nature varies, even within the same family. Some members may have tendencies like emotional vampirism, causing significant harm despite their outward moral behavior. This denial can leave children unprepared to handle the complexities of human behavior, making them vulnerable to manipulation and damage, as they lack the emotional armor needed to protect themselves.

Religious and Spiritual Beliefs:
Moral and Ethical Ideals

Religion and spirituality often promote high moral and ethical standards, such as compassion, forgiveness, individual responsibility. These teachings can reinforce unconscious idealism, particularly when they emphasize ideals without acknowledging the complexities of human behavior. For instance, a person taught to "turn the other cheek" might internalize the belief that they should always forgive and overlook others' faults, even at their own expense. This mindset can increase vulnerability to manipulation and covert bullying, potentially leading to broken dreams and financial ruin as they fail to recognize when others act with malicious intent.

The Role of Faith

Faith can contribute to unconscious idealism by encouraging individuals to believe in the fundamental goodness of humanity and the idea that everything happens for a reason. These beliefs can provide comfort and a sense of purpose, acting as a guiding light in challenging times. However, they can also lead to naivety. For instance, believing that "God has a plan" might cause someone to endure abusive relationships or harmful situations, thinking they are undergoing a test or that things will eventually work out for the best, which can lead to further harm and distress.

Cultural and Societal Narratives

Cultural and societal narratives significantly shape unconscious idealism. Stories, media, and traditions often depict idealized versions of life, love, and relationships, providing comfort and inspiration. For instance, fairy tales frequently portray good triumphing over evil, true love as perfect and everlasting, and families as unconditionally supportive. While these narratives can lead to unrealistic real-life expectations, they also provide hope and reassurance. As children grow into adults, these cultural ideals can become deeply embedded in their unconscious minds, influencing how they perceive and interact with the world.

Religious Superiority Through Idealism

Unconscious idealism, driven by the desire to align with divine virtues, often fosters a sense of moral superiority. From a religious standpoint, individuals may believe that by strictly adhering to virtues like kindness, patience, and humility, they can elevate their standing with God through the approval and admiration of others. For example, a person who believes that "being overly kind will make others favor them" might unconsciously adopt people-pleasing behaviors, viewing their actions as proof of their moral and spiritual excellence.

However, this sense of superiority may close their eyes to the more profound teachings of faith, which emphasize balance, self-respect, and discernment. In pursuing the moral high ground, they may overlook the imbalances in their relationships, continually giving but receiving little in return, thinking this sacrifice is a form of spiritual test or virtue. By embracing balance and discernment, they can empower themselves with self-respect and a deeper understanding of their worth in the eyes of others and God.

Educational and Social Conditioning

Schooling and Peer Influence

Educational environments and peer interactions significantly shape unconscious idealism. Schools often promote ideals such as fairness, cooperation, and academic excellence. While these values are essential, they can sometimes create unrealistic expectations. For example, the idea that "hard work always pays off" might lead people to believe that success is guaranteed if they just try hard enough, ignoring the roles of psychological background, luck, privilege, or systemic barriers. The need to fit in can solidify certain ideals, particularly during adolescence, a crucial period for developing one's identity and social values.

Societal Expectations

Societal expectations, including those related to gender roles, success, and social status, also contribute to the development of unconscious idealism. Society often imposes ideals about what it means to be a "good" person, a "successful" individual, or a "perfect" partner. While these expectations can create pressure to conform to certain ideals, they also provide a sense of accomplishment and pride when met. For instance, the societal ideal of the "self-sacrificing mother" can lead women to prioritize their family's needs over their own, even to the detriment of their health and well-being.

Idealism as a Defense Mechanism

Unconscious idealism often emerges as a defense mechanism in response to early trauma or adversity. By holding onto an idealized perception of the world, individuals create a psychological barrier that shields them from the harsh realities of their environment. However, when this idealism is recognized and confronted, it can become a driving force for personal growth and self-awareness.

For instance, a child raised in a dysfunctional or abusive household might develop a belief that their family is inherently 'good' because facing the painful truth is too overwhelming. This defense mechanism can carry into adulthood, making it difficult for them to recognize and address toxic behaviors within their family or other relationships. Yet, by acknowledging and challenging these idealized beliefs, they can embark on a journey toward healthier relationships and a more balanced understanding of the world.

THE PERPETUATION OF IDEALISM THROUGH REINFORCEMENT

The Burden of Validation

Positive feedback and validation often reinforce unconscious idealism. When individuals act according to their ideals and receive praise or approval, it strengthens their belief that these ideals are correct and beneficial. For instance, a person who is always generous and selfless might receive admiration from others, reinforcing their belief that putting others first is the "right" way to live. However, this can also set up a pattern where the individual feels compelled to continue acting according to their ideals, even when it is no longer healthy, psychologically, or financially sustainable.

The Imbalance of Energy Exchange and Its Psychological and Practical Impact

Covert bullying, marked by subtle manipulation and control, profoundly impacts targets by creating an imbalance in emotional and energetic exchange. Unlike overt bullying, it operates quietly, fostering self-doubt while leaving the target in a cycle of giving without reciprocation. This imbalance drains energy, disrupts relationships, and hinders personal and financial success, underscoring the importance of recognizing and addressing these dynamics.

Long-Term Effects

One of the most significant consequences of covert bullying is the development of an excessive need to please others, leading to a profound imbalance in energy exchange. This imbalance disrupts the natural give-and-take dynamic, trapping targets in a cycle of constant giving without sufficient support in return. Over time, this drains them emotionally and energetically.

Connection to Depression

This imbalance exhausts energy and exacerbates the target's emotional and psychological state. It creates the feeling of endlessly chasing harmony and mutual energy exchange, a pursuit that often leads to overwhelming frustration and emotional exhaustion. Unattained expectations and hopes eventually become a heavy psychological and energetic burden, contributing to feelings of despair and emotional stagnation.

Interpreting "Beware of the Evil of Those You Have Benefited" in the Context of Energy Imbalance

One of the most complex challenges for targets is their emotional and energetic attachment to individuals incapable of reciprocating their needs. This isn't necessarily because these individuals are inherently evil but because giving without receiving always creates an imbalance. The saying "Beware of the evil of those you have benefited" highlights how this "evil" often arises not from the receiver's nature but from the imbalance in energy dynamics.

When energy exchange is uneven, it often brings out the worst in the recipient toward the giver's generosity. The target eventually finds himself isolated and disappointed as the energy he has given becomes a source of frustration rather than a foundation for balanced and fulfilling relationships. For this reason, kind and generous people often find themselves socially and financially disadvantaged as they face recurring challenges in achieving balance and success in their lives.

How These Barriers Affect Financial and Personal Success

> Blocked Pathways to Success: The inability to build beneficial relationships or social networks that contribute to personal or professional growth.

Loss of Focus: Time and energy consumed by unbalanced relationships that could otherwise be directed toward achieving goals.

Reduced Motivation: Repeated disappointment from a lack of mutual energy exchange undermines the drive to accomplish tangible achievements.

Breaking the Cycle and Restoring Energy Balance

Targets must prioritize restoring their energy balance and redefining their approach to giving and receiving to escape this harmful pattern. The key steps to achieving this include:

Ending Unbalanced Relationships: Identifying relationships that drain their energy without return and reducing dependency on them.

Prioritizing Self-Healing: Strengthening oneself through meditation, therapy, and energy work is not just a suggestion; it's a crucial step in restoring energy balance. It's a way to show yourself the care and support you deserve and a path to healing that you don't have to walk alone. Building New Connections: Seeking relationships that promote balanced energy exchange.

Establishing Healthy Boundaries: Ensuring giving is intentional and thoughtful rather than driven by unconscious idealism.

The Path to Personal and Financial Success

Detaching from unbalanced relationships is a crucial step toward success. By reorganizing their energy, targets can discover:

> Renewed Creativity: The ability to focus on their goals rather than chasing the illusion of balanced exchanges.
>
> Supportive Relationships: Developing social networks that foster personal and professional growth.
>
> Self-Confidence: Regaining inner balance enhances their ability to make bold decisions to achieve their objectives.

Life and success hinge on energy balance. By confronting and eliminating these barriers, targets can unlock new opportunities and lead lives filled with harmony and abundance.

Unrealistic Expectations:

People with strong ideological beliefs might set unrealistic expectations for themselves and those around them, often resulting in disappointment, frustration, and a sense of failure when reality  doesn't measure up. For instance, an individual might assume their friends should always be supportive and loyal, overlooking that everyone has flaws and limitations. When these friends inevitably fail to meet such unspoken standards, the idealist may experience deep hurt and disillusionment.

Ignoring Practical Realities

Idealism can cause individuals to overlook the complexities and subtleties of real-life situations. By concentrating too much on how things ought to be, they might need to pay more attention to the practical actions required to reach their goals or overlook critical details that could lead to better solutions. In relationships, this could manifest as expecting a partner to meet all emotional needs or live up to an idealized version of love and commitment, setting unrealistic standards that strain the relationship.

Cognitive Dissonance:

The discomfort experienced when holding two conflicting beliefs—can also play a role in maintaining unconscious idealism. When an idealist encounters behavior that contradicts their beliefs, they may experience cognitive dissonance. To resolve this discomfort, they might rationalize the behavior or adjust their perception to fit their ideals rather than confronting the inconsistency. For example, if a friend betrays them, an idealist might convince themselves that the friend didn't mean any harm or that they did something to deserve the betrayal rather than acknowledging the friend's wrongdoing.

Strained Relationships

Unconscious idealism can strain relationships. Individuals may expect others to conform to their ideals without considering  their limitations, perspectives, or circumstances, leading to misunderstandings, conflict, resentment, and discord. In families, idealism might create rigid expectations about how family members should behave, often rooted in traditional or cultural beliefs. When reality doesn't match these ideals, it can cause significant emotional turmoil.

Perfectionism and Burnout: Pursuing perfection, driven by ideological beliefs, can result in chronic stress and burnout. Individuals may push themselves too hard, striving for an unattainable level of excellence, leading to mental and physical exhaustion. This relentless pursuit of perfection can also affect how individuals perceive themselves, leading to chronic self-criticism, anxiety, and a pervasive sense of inadequacy.

Lack of Flexibility: Idealistic thinking often involves rigid adherence to principles or goals, which can hinder adaptability. When circumstances change, individuals may struggle to adjust, clinging to their ideals rather than adapting to new realities. This inflexibility can be especially problematic in situations that require rapid adjustments and the capacity to respond to unexpected challenges.

Disillusionment: The gap between romantic expectations and reality can lead to profound disillusionment. Individuals may become cynical or disheartened when they realize their ideals are less achievable than imagined. This disillusionment can be particularly painful when it involves relationships, as the idealist might feel betrayed by people they once trusted.

Missed Opportunities: When individuals focus too much on an ideal outcome, they might overlook valuable opportunities that don't perfectly align with their vision, limiting growth, learning, and success in various aspects of life. For instance, someone might miss out on a fulfilling relationship because it doesn't meet their idealized criteria or turn down a career opportunity that aligns differently with their preconceived notions of success.

Oversimplification and Overlooked Ethical Dilemmas: Idealists tend to simplify complex issues, viewing them in black-and-white terms, which can lead to unrealistic solutions or ineffective actions. By failing to recognize the underlying complexities, they may expect others to change or behave in ways that align with their ideals. However, understanding the factors that shape real-world behavior, especially in relationships, is crucial to avoid this pitfall. It's crucial to strike a balance in our approach to moral or ethical dilemmas. Idealists may overlook the trade-offs and nuanced decisions required, leading to well-intentioned actions that inadvertently lead to negative consequences. By considering both the moral correctness and the potential harm their actions could cause, a more balanced and effective approach can be achieved.

Stunted Personal Growth: Individuals might avoid exploring alternative perspectives or acknowledging personal flaws when driven by unconscious idealism. This fixation on an idealized version of themselves or others can hinder self-reflection and personal growth. By failing to confront their imperfections or the complexities of life, they miss valuable opportunities for growth and self-improvement.

Overcommitment

Idealists may take on too many responsibilities or causes to live up to their ideals. This over-commitment can lead to being overwhelmed, stressed,

and unable to follow through on all their obligations, ultimately harming their effectiveness. They may find themselves stretched too thin, trying to meet everyone's expectations while neglecting their own needs.

Isolation: Idealists may need help to connect with people who don't share their views or meet their standards. As a result, they might judge others harshly or distance themselves from those who don't align with their ideals, leading to social isolation and strained relationships. Over time, this pattern can create a profound sense of loneliness and alienation.

Resistance to Change

Idealism can cause individuals to become deeply attached to particular visions or goals, making it challenging to accept

change or adjust to new information. This resistance to change can stunt personal growth and keep them from adopting more practical or effective strategies, potentially resulting in feeling stuck or lagging in a fast-paced, evolving environment.

Self-Sacrifice: In their quest to uphold certain ideals, individuals might overlook their own needs, well-being, or happiness. While this self-sacrifice can seem admirable, it often results in long-term health problems, emotional exhaustion, or diminished personal fulfillment. Over time, this can gradually wear down their sense of self, even as they feel proud of their perceived nobility or believe they are earning divine rewards. If they eventually realize the toll it has taken, it can lead to deep-seated resentment. If not, they may adopt a martyr-like role, continuing to sacrifice themselves without recognizing the harm it causes.

Moral Superiority

Unconscious idealism can lead individuals to develop a sense of moral superiority, where they believe their ideals are inherently better than those of others. This attitude often creates tension, judgment, and alienation in relationships, as they may appear self-righteous or inflexible. Over time, this behavior can further isolate them from others, preventing the formation of meaningful connections.

Financial and Material Losses: Pursuing ideals without considering practical implications can lead to financial or material losses. For example, an idealist might invest in a venture or cause without thoroughly assessing the risks, leading to significant setbacks. In the long term, this can result in a precarious financial situation that is difficult to recover from.

Overdependence on Idealistic Narratives

Idealists may rely too heavily on narratives or beliefs that align

with their ideals, even when evidence suggests otherwise. This overdependence can lead to poor decision-making, as idealists prioritize idealistic stories over facts or reality. It can also make them vulnerable to manipulation by those who exploit these narratives for their gain.

Difficulty in Accepting Imperfection

Idealism often drives individuals to pursue perfection in themselves, others, and the world around them. This pursuit can make it difficult for them to accept imperfections, leading to chronic dissatisfaction and an inability to appreciate progress or tiny victories. As a result, their happiness and well-being may gradually erode, leaving them in constant discontent.

The Trickle-Down Effect
Generational Curse & Breaking the Cycle

The impact of unconscious idealism is not limited to the individual, but it also has a profound effect on future generations. This creates a cycle where one generation's unresolved pain and unmet expectations are inherited by the next, leading to what is commonly referred to as a "generational curse". To break this cycle, it is crucial to bring these underlying beliefs and motivations to the surface. Recognizing the root causes of unconscious idealism—whether it stems from childhood injustice, favoritism, or past trauma—is the first step. This understanding can help individuals see how these unresolved issues shape their behaviors and expectations and guide them towards a healthier mindset.

Once these unconscious patterns are acknowledged, individuals can work toward healing and developing a more balanced approach to their ideals. Accepting that life is imperfect, that fairness isn't always attainable, and that relationships can be messy is a key step in breaking the cycle of unconscious idealism-driven tension. This realistic perspective enlightens individuals, allowing them to foster a more compassionate and flexible family environment, freeing future generations from the pressure of living under rigid ideals.

THE IMPACT OF FAMINEMIES & FRE-NEMIES
COVERT BULLYING

Covert bullying when perpetrated by those closest to the tar-

get—such as family members (faminemies, a portmanteau of 'family' and 'enemies' to denote relatives who engage in bullying behavior) or so-called friends (frenemies, a blend of 'friend' and 'enemy' to describe individuals who pretend to be friends but engage in bullying)—exerts a profound and pervasive influence that infiltrates every facet of a person's life.

This form of bullying is insidious, operating in subtle, often hidden ways that make it exceptionally challenging to recognize and even more difficult to confront. The psychological and physical toll of covert bullying can be severe, leading to deep-seated emotional wounds, chronic health issues, and, ultimately, shattered dreams. The damage inflicted by covert bullying creates a deep rift between the soul and the psyche, obstructing personal growth, fulfillment, and the ability to actualize one's true potential.

Psychological Impact

Erosion of Self-Worth and Identity

Covert bullying chips away at the target's self-worth and sense of identity. Through constant, subtle put-downs like 'you're not good enough' or 'you'll never succeed, gaslighting, and manipulation, the target begins to internalize negative beliefs about themselves. This erosion of self-esteem can lead to a distorted self-image where the individual feels inherently flawed, worthless, or undeserving of success and happiness. Over time, targets may lose touch with their true selves, adopting the negative identities imposed on them by their bullies, and that can result in a sense of lost identity, where targets struggle to understand who they are outside of the toxic narratives created by their abusers.

Procrastination and Self-Doubt

Procrastination is not simply a bad habit or a lack of motivation; it is often a loud, yet subtle manifestation of the emotional and psychological damage inflicted by covert bullying. This form of bullying, insidious by design, operates in the shadows, seeping into the target's psyche and leaving deep lasting wounds that are often misunderstood or overlooked. It's crucial to be hyper-aware of this insidious nature to protect oneself from its damaging effects.

This form of bullying is insidious by design, rooted in the bully's intent to instill self-doubt and undermine their target's confidence—the very confidence essential for success. The bully's ultimate aim is to sabotage their target's ability to achieve their potential. This can be achieved through subtle tactics such as veiled criticisms, dismissive comments, or manipulation. Each postponed task becomes a painful reminder of internal struggles, amplifying feelings of inadequacy and unworthiness. Over time, this pattern becomes deeply ingrained, trapping targets in a cycle of procrastination that robs them of opportunities for growth, success, and self-fulfillment.

Targets often struggle to succeed in business or personal ventures, sensing an inexplicable force holding them back. They may pour time and energy into various strategies but feel like they are hitting an invisible wall, an insurmountable barrier that prevents them from moving forward. This unrecognized burden feeds procrastination, creating a vicious cycle of frustration, hesitation, and self-sabotage.

What makes this struggle even more devastating is that most targets remain unaware of the covert bully's impact on their lives. In their search for answers, some turn to unconventional solutions, such as consulting spiritual practitioners, convinced they are cursed or blocked by an external force. Ironically, their intuition is partially correct—but not in the way they imagine. The "block" they feel is not the result of mystical interference but rather the cumulative effect of a psychological war waged against them.

Breaking free from this cycle requires understanding its roots, acknowledging the impact of covert bullying, and taking deliberate steps to reclaim confidence and self-worth. Understanding the problem's origins is not just the first step but a powerful tool for taking control of your life and your future.

Psychological Paralysis

Trapped in the "No-Time Zone"

Targets of covert bullying often find themselves in a state of psychological paralysis; they feel stuck and unable to move forward, usually convincing themselves they will have more energy, clarity, or confidence to take action tomorrow. This belief, while comforting at the moment, keeps them suspended in a timeless limbo, oblivious to the fact that life is too short to postpone their potential endlessly. But there is hope. Breaking free from this cycle brings a sense of relief and renewed optimism for the future.

This paralysis is akin to being stuck in quicksand. The more targets try to rationalize or plan their way out, the deeper they sink. They reassure themselves that tomorrow holds the answer and that they will act when they feel more ready. Yet, "tomorrow" rarely comes, leaving them immobilized. Over time, the quicksand of inaction swallows them whole, erasing their dreams and preventing their potential from materializing.

Targets of covert bullying are often unaware of how the psychological wounds inflicted by their bullies create this state. Subtle manipulation veiled criticisms, and the deliberate instillation of self-doubt leave them in this "no-time zone," drowning in hesitation and indecision. The tragedy lies not only in the wasted time but in the unfulfilled potential—the life of growth, achievement, and fulfillment that could have been.

The Perfectionism Trap

Targets of covert bullying often develop perfectionistic tendencies as a way to cope with feelings of inadequacy. They set unattainable standards, believing that only perfection can validate their worth. This mindset creates an obsessive need to redo tasks repeatedly, often without a clear purpose or direction. Their thoughts become like a treadmill—constantly running yet leading nowhere. While perfectionism may initially appear as a commitment to excellence, it quickly becomes self-defeating. The relentless pursuit of flawlessness consumes time and energy yet fails to bring meaningful progress toward goals. Over time, the fear of falling short becomes paralyzing, leading to procrastination. Tasks are delayed not due to laziness but because the perceived risk of failure feels too overwhelming to face.

The Impatience Dilemma

Impatience often accompanies perfectionism, adding another layer of complexity for targets. They expect instant, dramatic results, bypassing the foundational steps necessary for long-term success. This impatience can lead to procrastination, as targets may delay tasks, hoping to achieve a more immediate, perfect result. Like trying to run before learning to crawl, they must pay more attention to gradual progress and consistent effort.

This impatience breeds frustration when success takes time to come. Instead of focusing on steady, incremental growth, they become consumed by obsessing over details to keep their minds occupied. They mistakenly equate "being busy" with achieving success, failing to realize that true success begins from within, fueled by clarity, purpose, and aligned action.

This anxious, desperate energy prevents meaningful progress and repels people, opportunities, and wealth. The key to breaking free from this destructive cycle is cultivating inner peace, setting clear goals, and channeling efforts into purposeful, consistent action. Success is not achieved by frantic, aimless activity but by pairing a calm, centered mindset with deliberate, focused work.

Fear and Ridicule

At the core of this paralysis lies a deep fear of exposure. Targets of covert bullying often worry that their efforts will unveil their perceived inadequacies, playing directly into the bully's negative narrative. This fear is not just about failure; it is compounded by the dread of humiliation and ridicule, which the bully subtly reinforces. Often underestimated, this fear becomes a powerful force that perpetuates the damaging effects of covert bullying. It leads targets to avoid action, convincing themselves they will act "later" when they feel more prepared or confident. However, this elusive "later" rarely comes. Instead, it leaves a trail of unfulfilled potential, missed opportunities, and the persistent shadow of what could have been.

Self-Erosion and Procrastination long term

The psychological damage caused by covert bullying leads to a profound erosion of self-belief, ultimately manifesting as procrastination. Over time, veiled insults, dismissive comments, and subtle manipulation chip away at a target's confidence. These seemingly minor attacks accumulate, leaving a devastating impact on the target's psyche. As targets internalize the belief that they are flawed or incapable, hesitation and second-guessing become constant companions. A persistent fear of failure takes root, and procrastination emerges as a protective mechanism. By avoiding tasks or decisions, targets attempt to shield themselves from the risk of judgment and inadequacy. This "procrastination vibe" creates an aura of stagnation, locking them into cycles of avoidance and indecision.

This paralysis often spans years, preventing targets from pursuing careers, relationships, or personal goals. They may only recognize the extent of their lost opportunities later in life, grappling with deep regret for the dreams left unrealized. The paralyzing combination of procrastination, perfectionism, and self-doubt keeps them from reaching their full potential, reinforcing their belief that success is out of reach.

Understanding this cycle of self-erosion and its long-term effects is crucial for building empathy and offering support. Breaking free requires recognizing the root causes, reclaiming self-worth, and taking deliberate steps to rebuild confidence and take meaningful action.

Chronic Anxiety and Hypervigilance

The constant psychological manipulation inherent in covert bullying leads to a state of chronic anxiety. Targets often find themselves on high alert, perpetually anxious about the next subtle attack or undermining comment. This hypervigilance is exhausting and can lead to significant mental health issues, such as generalized anxiety disorder (GAD) or panic disorder. The fear of constant betrayal or manipulation leads to withdrawal and isolation. Even in seemingly safe environments, the residual anxiety from past experiences with covert bullies can prevent targets from fully engaging or forming new, healthy relationships.

Depression and Emotional Numbing

As covert bullying continues, many targets develop depression, characterized by persistent sadness, hopelessness, and a lack of interest in activities they once enjoyed. The emotional toll of being consistently undermined and manipulated can sap a person's will to engage with life, leading to a state of emotional numbness or apathy. This depression can be further exacerbated by the target's isolation from support systems, as covert bullying often involves tactics that drive wedges between the target and their friends, family, or colleagues. This isolation deepens depression, creating a cycle that is difficult to break.

Complex Post-Traumatic Stress Disorder (C-PTSD)

Complex Post-Traumatic Stress Disorder (C-PTSD) is distinct from PTSD, which often develops after a single traumatic incident. C-PTSD, on the other hand, emerges from continuous and repeated emotional abuse, such as covert bullying. Targets of C-PTSD endure a relentless cycle of trauma that is far more insidious, as it stems from continuous emotional harm rather than a one-time incident.

Individuals suffering from C-PTSD endure a relentless cycle of trauma that is far more insidious, as it stems from continuous emotional harm rather than a one-time incident. They experience recurring flashbacks, intense emotional turmoil, and significant challenges in regulating their emotions. The ongoing trauma traps them in a vicious loop, where they constantly relive their painful experiences, making it exceedingly difficult to progress and move forward in their lives. This state of being perpetually on edge, combined with the overthinking and analyzing of what went wrong, can lead to severe psychological distress.

One of the most debilitating effects of C-PTSD is dissociation, a mental disconnection from reality that targets often resort to as a coping mechanism. This dissociation can profoundly impact their ability to stay present in their daily lives, affecting everything from their performance at work and school to their relationships. The constant struggle to manage overwhelming emotions while feeling detached from reality exacerbates their sense of isolation and helplessness, creating a significant barrier to healing and recovery.

Addiction and Compulsive Behaviors

Covert bullying targets often seek refuge in addictive behaviors as a form of escape from their emotional pain. Substance abuse, including drugs and alcohol, can become a temporary crutch that provides relief but ultimately leads to physical health deterioration, strained relationships, and financial instability.

Food addiction is another typical response, where targets turn to an obsession with food to numb their feelings or regain a sense of control, often resulting in various eating disorders. Similarly, some may develop sex addiction, using sexual encounters as a way to feel desired or valued, even if only temporarily, which can lead to a damaged self-image, social issues, and physical harm.

Shopping addiction is also prevalent among those affected by covert bullying. Targets may impulsively purchase items in an attempt to find comfort in material possessions, using shopping as a temporary way to ease their emotional turmoil. However, this behavior often spirals into a cycle of financial instability and guilt, trapping them in a pattern of compulsive spending and regret.

Obsessive Thinking

It is another form of compulsive behavior that can take hold, where targets constantly replay negative interactions in their minds, trying to understand or predict future attacks. This obsessive thinking can become all-consuming, leaving little room for positive or productive thoughts. Anger can manifest as a result of covert bullying either turned inward, leading to self-destructive behaviors such as self-harm or substance abuse, or outward, causing problems in personal and professional relationships. This anger is often a response to the perceived loss of control over one's life, and without proper outlets, it can lead to further psychological damage.

Emotional Immaturity

Covert bullying forces the brain to navigate a maze of confu-

sion and emotional manipulation, leading to a troubling consequence: self-gaslighting. As targets try to make sense of the injustice they face, they begin doubting their perceptions, questioning whether their feelings and responses are valid. They convince themselves they are overreacting or misunderstanding the situation. This pattern of self-doubt eventually becomes a survival tactic. To protect itself from ongoing psychological assault, the brain starts invalidating the target's experiences to prevent further conflict or confusion. Instead of recognizing the emotional abuse, targets rationalize it, telling themselves, "It's not that bad" or "It's all in my head." Over time, this internal denial prevents them from acknowledging the full extent of the abuse.

This mental conflict, where targets recognize the abuse but simultaneously downplay its severity, stunts their emotional growth. By gaslighting themselves, targets remain emotionally immature, unable to process their pain. Rather than developing healthy ways to manage conflict and protect their well-being, they fall into self-blame and emotional suppression.

This lack of emotional development leaves targets feeling powerless and unsure of how to advocate for their needs. They struggle to trust their instincts and make decisions because their inner voice becomes clouded by the bully's manipulative narratives. As this emotional paralysis deepens, targets lose the ability to confront challenges, leading to long-term psychological harm and stunted personal growth.

IMPACT ON ROMANTIC ATTACHMENT STYLES

The Search for Validation

Covert bullying inflicts profound emotional distress, leaving targets with an emotional void that often leads them to seek validation from others. According to attachment theory, secure attachments develop in love, safety, and support environments. However, targets of covert bullying frequently develop insecure attachment styles—either anxious or avoidant—due to the emotional manipulation and gaslighting they experience. These attachment styles significantly affect their ability to form healthy, balanced relationships.

Anxious Attachment

The Desperate Search for Approval

People with anxious attachment intensely need validation and overwhelming fear rejection, Covert bullying and overwhelming fear rejection as it often strips away target's self-worth causing them to develop this attachment style and become emotionally dependent on others for security. They continuously seek reassurance in romantic, familial, or professional relationships by over-accommodating and compromising their needs to avoid conflict or abandonment.

In non-romantic relationships, such as friendships and workplace environments, this attachment style manifests as excessive people-pleasing or fear of asserting their boundaries. Targets tolerate toxic or one-sided relationships to avoid rejection. This constant need for approval creates imbalanced dynamics, leaving targets emotionally drained and trapped in relationships that do not truly value them.

Example of Anxious Attachment

Scenario: Romantic Relationship

Sarah and John have been dating for a year. Due to the covert bullying Sarah experienced growing up, she developed an anxious attachment style, which affects her relationship with John. Sarah constantly seeks reassurance from him, frequently asking questions like, 'Do you still love me?' or 'Are you upset with me?' When John doesn't immediately respond with the reassurance she craves, Sarah assumes he's losing interest, which only fuels her anxiety.

At the same time, to avoid pushing John away, Sarah often suppresses her needs and compromises her boundaries to keep him happy. Even when uncomfortable, she remains silent, fearing that expressing her true feelings might lead to conflict or rejection. This leaves her feeling emotionally unfulfilled, but she stays quiet, believing preserving the relationship is necessary.

Over time, John becomes overwhelmed by Sarah's constant need for validation and inability to voice her true needs. Although he cares for her, he finds her emotional intensity exhausting and begins to pull away. The very behavior Sarah engages in to avoid losing John — her anxious need for reassurance and suppression of her own needs — ironically makes her less attractive to him. As their relationship imbalance grows, the emotional wedge between them deepens. Eventually, John distances himself completely. Sarah's fear of abandonment, deeply rooted in her anxious attachment style, becomes a self-fulfilling prophecy, driving John away and leaving her heartbroken and alone.

Avoidant Attachment
Emotional Withdrawal and Self-Reliance

On the other end of the spectrum, some targets of covert bullying develop an avoidant attachment style. Instead of seeking validation from others, they distance themselves emotionally, prioritizing self-reliance over emotional closeness. Shaped by covert bullying, these individuals withdraw from deep relationships to protect themselves from vulnerability and emotional harm, as the bullying erodes their trust in others for emotional support, ultimately leading to isolation.

The emotional harm caused by covert bullying is significant and cannot be underestimated. While they may avoid seeking validation, they are not immune to the effects of covert bullying. By keeping relationships at a surface level, they shield themselves from the emotional risks of deeper connections. Still, in doing so, they hinder their ability to form genuine bonds and experience authentic intimacy.

Example of Avoidant Attachment

Scenario: Family and Social Relationships

Mark grew up in a family where covert bullying was prevalent. As a result, he developed an avoidant attachment style. In his family, sharing emotions often led to manipulation or judgment, so Mark learned to withdraw to protect himself emotionally. As an adult, Mark maintains surface-level relationships with family and friends. He rarely shares his feelings and avoids deep emotional conversations, preferring to keep interactions light. Mark's colleagues see him as competent and independent at work, but he seldom participates in team-building activities or social gatherings.

Although Mark justifies his emotional withdrawal as self-protection, his distance prevents him from forming meaningful friendships. While he appears self-sufficient, his avoidant attachment style leaves him feeling isolated and misses out on the deeper connections that could bring fulfillment.

Covert Bullying Impact on Anxious and Avoidant Attachment Styles

Both anxious and avoidant attachment styles disrupt all types of relationships, creating significant emotional imbalances. Those with anxious attachment are often seen as overly dependent or needy, constantly seeking approval. On the other hand, avoidant individuals are perceived as emotionally detached or uninterested. These dynamics strain romantic, familial, or professional relationships, highlighting the urgent need to address these issues.

People with anxious attachments may exhaust those around them with their constant need for reassurance, while avoidant individuals may appear distant, leading to misunderstandings and emotional gaps. Both attachment styles ultimately reinforce the sense of worthlessness instilled by covert bullying, trapping targets in unhealthy relationship patterns.

Rejection and Its Emotional Toll

Rejection is particularly devastating for targets of covert bully-

ing. Those with anxious attachment may respond by obsessively pursuing the person who rejected them, unable to accept the disconnection. In contrast, avoidant individuals tend to retreat further into emotional withdrawal, their belief that vulnerability only leads to pain reinforced with each rejection.

Rejection can have a profound and destructive emotional im-

pact, sometimes leading to depression, self-harm thoughts, or self-destructive behaviors. Targets remain trapped in a cycle of rejection and feelings of inadequacy, struggling to free themselves from its psychological effects.

The Lesser of Two Evils
Avoidant Attachment and Social Perception
Balancing Anxious and Avoidant Attachments
in Social Contexts

Covert bullying, such as exclusion from social groups or spreading rumors, can lead to both anxious and avoidant attachment styles. However, avoidant attachment is often perceived as less harmful in social settings. Individuals with avoidant attachment are seen as more emotionally independent, which serves as a defense mechanism to shield themselves from the potential pain of rejection. This perceived self-reliance enhances their respect in society, making them appear self-sufficient.

While avoidant attachment is accompanied by isolation, it of-

ten protects social status and preserves respect. In contrast, anxious attachment manifests in behaviors such as constant approval-seeking, compromising personal boundaries, and excessive emotional dependence, which can undermine the target's social standing. These behaviors increase the likelihood of rejection and loss of status.

Consequently, avoidant attachment may offer greater social protection despite its emotional limitations compared to anxious attachment, which exposes targets to negative social judgment. However, while avoidant attachment may appear less socially damaging, it conceals deep emotional pain. Unlike anxious individuals, who outwardly express their struggles, avoidant individuals internalize their pain, often grappling with intense sadness, loneliness, and feelings of worthlessness. This internalized suffering can become overwhelming, placing them at a heightened risk of severe mental health issues, including suicidal thoughts. Understanding and empathy are crucial when dealing with individuals struggling with avoidant attachment.

By withdrawing emotionally and avoiding deep relationships, individuals with avoidant attachment protect themselves from rejection but also deprive themselves of meaningful connections. This emotional distance provides the illusion of independence and shields them from direct hurt, yet it leaves them in isolation and profound emptiness. They frequently feel that life lacks vitality and meaning, existing in a self-imposed cycle of avoidance and solitude, which prevents them from truly engaging with life and deepening their relationships.

Breaking the Cycle
Rebuilding Self-Worth in Relationships

To break free from insecure attachment cycles, targets of covert bullying must focus on rebuilding their self-worth from within. This journey requires acknowledging and healing the emotional wounds caused by bullying through therapy, mindfulness, and self-compassion. Self-compassion, the practice of being kind and understanding toward oneself, particularly in the face of personal failure or inadequacy, is vital to the healing process. It helps targets reduce their dependence on others for validation and fosters healthier relationships.

Regaining self-worth is the foundation for emotional independence and healing. By shifting from seeking external approval to nurturing inner growth, targets can build secure, meaningful relationships where they are valued and respected. Through self-compassion and inner strength, they can break the cycle of emotional dependency and create balanced, healthy connections across all areas of life.

Physical Health Consequences

Covert bullying affects both the mind and body because its hidden nature forces the body to internalize stress without a proper outlet, leading to physical symptoms like skin problems and other illnesses. Recognizing these physical signs is essential to understanding the link between emotional and physical health. This awareness promotes a more holistic approach to healing, offering those affected by covert bullying the comprehensive support they need on their path to recovery and emotional well-being.

Psychosomatic Illnesses: The stress from covert bullying can also manifest as psychosomatic illnesses, where physical symptoms have no identifiable medical cause but are very real to the target. Common psychosomatic symptoms include chronic pain, headaches, and muscle tension. These symptoms are real and directly result from the body's response to psychological stress. For many targets, these psychosomatic illnesses can be just as debilitating as physical conditions with a precise medical diagnosis. The lack of a clear medical cause can lead to frustration and despair, as targets may feel that their pain is not taken seriously by healthcare providers or their social circle, and that can lead to a sense of isolation and helplessness, as targets feel misunderstood and unsupported in their struggle.

Gastrointestinal Disorders: Psychological stress and anxiety caused by covert bullying can have a severe impact on the digestive system, leading to a range of gastrointestinal issues. The digestive system is often referred to as the "second brain" due to its extensive network of neurons and neurotransmitters that communicate directly with the brain via the vagus nerve. This nerve creates a two-way pathway, allowing constant signal exchange between the brain and the gut, with each influencing the other.

Stress stimulates the vagus nerve, which can alter gut motility and secretions, explaining why stress and anxiety often manifest as cramps, bloating, and stomach pain. The gut is highly sensitive to emotional shifts, reacting to psychological stress with noticeable physiological changes.

Those experiencing chronic stress frequently develop conditions such as irritable bowel syndrome (IBS), acid reflux, ulcers, and bloating. These conditions aren't just inconvenient; they can be debilitating, with physical symptoms directly tied to the target's emotional state, often flaring up during heightened anxiety or stress. For many, these gastrointestinal issues become chronic, significantly diminishing their quality of life. The severity of pain and discomfort may even limit their ability to engage in daily activities, furthering their social isolation and emotional distress. The ongoing struggle with physical illness, combined with psychological strain, creates a difficult cycle of suffering that is hard to break.

Cardiovascular Problems: The prolonged stress response associated with covert bullying is also a significant risk factor for cardiovascular issues. Chronic stress triggers the continuous release of stress hormones, like cortisol, which can cause lasting damage to the heart and blood vessels. Over time, this can lead to serious cardiovascular conditions, including hypertension, heart disease, and even heart attacks. Targets who lack effective ways to manage stress are particularly at risk, leaving their bodies in a constant state of fight-or-flight.

Targets often experience physical symptoms such as palpitations, chest pain, or shortness of breath. These symptoms, which may mimic cardiovascular events, heighten their anxiety and create a harmful cycle where physical stress exacerbates psychological distress, which in turn further impacts the body. As a result, targets can feel trapped, unable to escape the combined effects of their psychological and physical suffering.

Autoimmune Disorders and Chronic Illnesses: Persistent stress triggers and worsens autoimmune disorders, causing the immune system to attack the body's tissues mistakenly. Prolonged stress from covert bullying can lead to or intensify conditions like lupus, rheumatoid arthritis, and multiple sclerosis. Conditions such as lupus, rheumatoid arthritis, and multiple sclerosis can be triggered or worsened by the relentless stress of covert bullying.

These diseases are not only physically debilitating but also emotionally draining, as targets may experience flare-ups during periods of high stress, further complicating their physical health and reducing their ability to manage their daily lives.

The physical limitations imposed by these diseases can lead to a sense of helplessness and further erosion of self-esteem. Targets may feel as though their bodies are betraying them, compounding the emotional pain inflicted by the bullying. The intersection of physical and psychological suffering can make it incredibly difficult for targets to maintain hope or motivation, trapping them in a cycle of despair.

Eating Disorders and Body Dysmorphia: Covert bullying that focuses on a target's appearance can be especially harmful, often resulting in the development of Disordered eating behaviors such as anorexia, bulimia, binge eating, or body dysmorphia. Targets may engage in disordered eating behaviors as a means of exerting control over their lives or as a response to body shaming or criticism. These eating disorders are serious mental health conditions that can lead to severe physical health problems, including malnutrition, heart problems, and even death. In addition to eating disorders, targets may also develop body dysmorphia, a condition where individuals obsess over perceived flaws in their appearance.

This obsessive focus on body image can lead to extreme distress and often requires intensive psychological therapy to address. The psychological strain of constantly worrying about one's appearance can take a significant toll on both mental and physical health, leading to social withdrawal, depression, and a further erosion of self-esteem.

The Impact of Covert Bullying on Weight Gain: Covert bullying, with its subtle and manipulative tactics, creates long-term emotional stress for targets. The continuous stress from covert bullying keeps the body on high alert, causing it to produce excess cortisol, a hormone linked to stress regulation. Over time, elevated cortisol levels can stimulate appetite, often leading to cravings for foods that are high in calories, sugar, and fat. The long-term effects of this stress are concerning and should motivate us to address the issue.

As a result, individuals may find themselves eating more than usual or turning to comfort foods as a way to cope with emotional pain. This is a natural response to the stress caused by covert bullying. Over time, this shift in eating habits can lead to the body storing excess fat, especially around the abdomen, which is a typical response to prolonged stress. The weight gain becomes not just a physical issue, but also an emotional one, further diminishing self-esteem and creating a cycle of stress and unhealthy behaviors. For targets of covert bullying, the emotional toll can slowly transform into visible weight gain, adding another layer of difficulty in the recovery process.

The Impact of Covert Bullying on Aging

Our study on the effects of covert bullying on aging is vital because it highlights an important yet frequently neglected dimension of mental health. Covert bullying can accelerate the aging process, both physically and mentally, due to the prolonged emotional stress it causes. When someone experiences chronic stress, as is often the case with covert bullying, their body remains in a heightened state of tension, continuously releasing stress hormones like cortisol. This constant release of cortisol has damaging effects on the body, especially the skin.

As these proteins break down, the skin loses its resilience, leading to the appearance of wrinkles and sagging, which are early signs of aging. Prolonged stress also hampers the body's ability to heal and regenerate, further accelerating the aging process. For targets of covert bullying, this can manifest as prematurely aged skin and diminished energy levels, reflecting the weight of their emotional distress.

Understanding these implications can help healthcare professionals and individuals alike to be more aware and prepared to deal with the effects of covert bullying on aging. Cortisol, produced in response to stress, can damage collagen and elastin—proteins that help the skin stay firm and elastic.

The Hidden Physical Impact of Covert Bullying
How Stress Affects the Skin

Many people overlook how emotional distress can significantly impact the skin, one of the most sensitive indicators of our mental state. Recognizing these signs in our skin can empower us to take control of our emotional and physical well-being. Continuous exposure to covert bullying leads to persistent stress and anxiety, causing the body to remain in a heightened state of alert. This prompts the release of cortisol, a hormone that manages stress. While cortisol is beneficial for handling short-term stress, prolonged release—especially in family settings—can disrupt the body's natural functions and contribute to skin issues.

Common Skin Issues Linked to Stress from Covert Bullying

Acne Breakouts: Stress increases oil production, which clogs pores and leads to acne, compounding emotional distress during challenging times.

Eczema and Psoriasis: Ongoing stress weakens the immune system, making flare-ups of eczema and psoriasis more frequent and severe, leading to dry, itchy, and inflamed skin.

Hives and Rashes: Emotional pressure can trigger the body to release histamines, causing hives or rashes as a physical reaction to stress.

Rosacea Flare-ups: Anxiety and social stress can worsen rosacea, increasing redness and facial inflammation during heightened emotional strain.

The Emotional-Skin Cycle

The relationship between stress and skin conditions often becomes a harmful cycle. As individuals, we have the power to break this cycle. By addressing the stress from covert bullying and its impact on our skin, we can take proactive steps towards healing, both emotionally and physically.

The Mind-Body Connection

Psychodermatology, the study of the relationship between emotions and skin health, reveals how stress from covert bullying can directly impact the skin. Our skin often acts as a visible expression of emotional stress, showing signs of internal turmoil. Recognizing this connection is essential for promoting both emotional healing and physical wellness.

Healing the Skin by Addressing Emotional Roots

The skin often reflects emotional pain. For those suffering from covert bullying, conditions like acne, rashes, and inflammation may be physical expressions of internal distress.

The emotional and physical impacts of bullying must be addressed to have clear skin. Emotional trauma disrupts the body's balance, exacerbating skin problems. By focusing on emotional recovery through therapy, mindfulness, or self-compassion, individuals can also experience improvements in their skin. As emotional wounds heal, physical symptoms tend to lessen, offering a path to both mental and physical recovery.

Financial Consequences

Reduced Career Advancement and Job Stability: The impact of covert bullying on a person's mental health can have significant consequences for their career progression. Targets may feel unworthy of promotions or hesitant to apply for better positions, leading to career stagnation. Persistent self-doubt and fear of failure may lead to overlooked opportunities. Targets may avoid taking risks or advocating for themselves in the workplace. Additionally, the mental and physical health issues caused by bullying can lead to absenteeism, decreased productivity, or even job loss.

Targets may struggle to maintain consistent employment, leading to financial instability and difficulty building a stable career. Over time, this can result in long-term financial insecurity, as targets find themselves unable to achieve their professional goals or secure a comfortable standard of living.

Increased Medical Expenses*:* The physical health problems caused by covert bullying often require extensive medical attention, leading to increased healthcare costs. Frequent visits to doctors, hospitalizations, and ongoing treatment for chronic conditions such as autoimmune diseases or cardiovascular is-sues can create a substantial financial burden.

These medical expenses can become overwhelming for tar-gets without adequate health insurance, potentially leading to significant debt. The financial strain of managing chronic health conditions can exacerbate the target's stress and anxi-ety, creating a cycle of economic and emotional distress that is difficult to escape. The burden of medical bills can also lead to tough decisions, such as choosing between paying for neces-sary treatment and covering other essential expenses, further compounding the target's sense of helplessness.

Impaired Financial Decision Making: The stress and anxiety from covert bullying can also impair a target's ability to make sound financial decisions. Targets may make impulsive pur-chases as a coping mechanism, using shopping or other forms of consumption to relieve their emotional pain temporarily. However, these impulsive decisions can lead to financial insta-bility, as targets may find themselves struggling to manage their money effectively. Additionally, the constant stress and anxiety can cloud judgment, making it difficult for targets to plan for the future or make critical financial decisions. Over time, this impaired decision-making can lead to a cycle of fi-nancial insecurity that is hard to break, leaving targets trapped in economic instability.

Long-Term Financial Dependency: As targets of covert bul-lying struggle with the psychological and physical impacts of their abuse, they may become financially dependent on others, particularly if their ability to work is compromised. This dependency can perpetuate feelings of helplessness and reduce their ability to break free from toxic environments. Financial dependency can also lead to further manipulation by the covert bully, who may use financial control to maintain power over the target; this can lead to a repetitive cycle of mistreatment, making the target feel stuck and unable to escape. They cannot escape their circumstances due to their financial reliance on the bully.

Energy Blocks and Unfulfilled Potential: Covert bullying often creates psychological barriers or "energy blocks" that prevent individuals from fully realizing their potential. These blocks can manifest as procrastination, fear of failure, or an inability to commit to long-term goals, leaving targets unable to pursue their passions or achieve their dreams. These energy blocks mainly affect individuals with significant potential. Despite having the skills, knowledge, and ambition to succeed, they find themselves stuck, unable to break free from the limitations imposed by their psychological state. This unfulfilled potential translates into lost opportunities, both personally and financially, as targets cannot achieve the success, they are capable of.

BAD LUCK

THE HIDDEN CURSE OF COVERT BULLYING

Good Luck: is Alignment of the Soul & Psyche, it doesn't just come from external circumstances or chance but from the internal harmony between the soul and psyche. People navigate life with clarity, resilience, and confidence when the inner self and mind are aligned. This alignment allows them to make decisions that reflect their true desires, pursue goals with conviction, and attract positive outcomes. Covert bullying severely disrupts the connection between the target's soul and psyche. Manipulation, gaslighting, and consistent undermining erode self-trust, intuition, and confidence, creating internal conflict. As a result, targets misinterpret the chaos in their lives as bad luck when it is, in fact, a manifestation of their fractured internal state.

The Impact of Covert Bullying
The Curse of Bad Luck

When psychological trauma from covert bullying remains unresolved, the target's life begins to spiral into patterns of perceived rotten luck. Internally, emotional wounds become invisible barriers that block personal growth, erode resilience, and hinder success. Externally, these wounds manifest as setbacks in relationships, finances, and careers, all mistakenly attributed to misfortune.

The Attraction to Toxic Relationships

Covert bullying disrupts targets' self-worth, causing them to enter toxic relationships that mirror their diminished sense of self. Conditioned by years of emotional manipulation, they believe they are undeserving of love, which leads them to attract partners or friends who exploit this weakness. In these relationships, targets may feel manipulated, drained, and emotionally abused, which reinforces the belief that they are unlucky in love, which creates a vicious cycle. Each failed relationship convinces the target that they are doomed to bad luck in their connections. However, the actual cause is the unresolved trauma that guides them toward toxic relationships, leaving them trapped in unhealthy emotional patterns.

Financial Exploitation: A Cycle of Loss

In financial matters, targets of covert bullying experience similar patterns of exploitation. Their damaged sense of self-worth makes them doubt their value and undercut themselves in business, leaving them vulnerable to manipulative business partners, dishonest friends, or toxic family members. They might settle for less in negotiations, fail to assert themselves, or allow others to take advantage of their hard work. This self-sabotage in financial matters leads to repeated financial losses and missed opportunities. The target, believing they are unlucky in money, fails to see that their unresolved trauma and lack of self-advocacy perpetuate these patterns. Without healing their internal wounds, the financial setbacks they experience will continue to feel like bad luck.

Self-Sabotage

The Unconscious Reinforcement of Bad Luck

One of the most insidious ways covert bullying perpetuates the illusion of bad luck is through self-sabotage. Targets of covert bullying often unconsciously undermine their success. They procrastinate, fear failure, and shy away from fully committing to their goals. Their belief that they are undeserving of success, deeply embedded through years of manipulation, leads them to hesitate, retreat, or avoid pursuing growth opportunities. This self-sabotage creates a cycle of disappointment. Even when presented with chances for progress, targets hold themselves back, reinforcing the belief that they are unlucky. In reality, it is the psychological scars of covert bullying that prevent them from stepping into their full potential.

- ## The Role of Subconscious Conditioning

The notion of "bad luck" can be traced back to the subconscious conditioning that covert bullying ingrains in its targets. Gaslighting, emotional manipulation, and subtle psychological abuse create deep-seated beliefs that targets are undeserving of success, love, or happiness. These subconscious beliefs drive their actions, leading them to experience failure or exploitation. When setbacks occur, targets of covert bullying may not recognize that their decisions, shaped by years of psychological abuse, are leading them toward these outcomes. They cannot break free because their subconscious mind has normalized failure and disappointment, leading them to interpret these patterns as unlucky.

A Chaotic Life: Internal and External Disorder

Covert bullying affects more than just relationships and finances, often showing up in targets' physical environments. Internally, unresolved emotional trauma creates chaos, self-doubt, and confusion. This internal disorder usually spills into their external world, creating disorganized, cluttered living environments that mirror the internal chaos they experience. Their homes may become disordered, full of clutter, or lacking structure, symbolizing their psychological state. As their mental and emotional state continues to unravel, so does their ability to maintain order in their lives. This external chaos further feeds their sense of bad luck, as the disarray in their surroundings reinforces the belief that their life is out of control.

The "Oh, Poor You" Effect: Covert Bullying's Insidious Impact

The 'Oh, poor you' effect is a manipulative tactic where the

bully creates chaos in the target's life while feigning sympathy. Covert bullies lead their targets into psychological disarray, causing them to feel utterly lost and confused due to the emotional damage inflicted. This emotional turmoil, often overlooked, is a crucial part of the target's experience. The manipulation often extends to financial ruin, as the bully sabotages opportunities, undermines the target's credibility, and turns others against them. The covert bully's goal is to isolate the target and ruin their reputation to the point where other 'wannabe bullies' join in, viewing the target as weak or incapable.

This chain reaction leads to unfulfilled potential and financial ruins which is the ultimate aim of the bully.

The long-term impact of this manipulation is concerning and should motivate us to take action against it. What makes this manipulation especially cruel is the covert bully's ability to appear concerned, often offering false pity while pretending to feel "bad" for the target. This dynamic mirrors historical Arabic proverbs such as "Kill a man and go cry at his funeral," highlighting the insidious nature of their tactics. The covert bully damages, isolates, and destroys while maintaining a façade of concern and sympathy, deepening the target's despair and entrapment.

BREAKING THE CYCLE
REBUILDING THE
CONNECTION BETWEEN SOUL & PSYCHE

Healing from the trauma of covert bullying requires more than external strategies. It involves realigning the soul and psyche, rebuilding self-worth, and reestablishing trust in one's instincts. Through this deep internal healing, targets can break free from the illusion of bad luck.

Targets rebuild their inner connection and gain the clarity, resilience, and confidence needed to make empowered choices. This realignment helps them attract healthier relationships, seize financial opportunities, and restore order. The perceived lousy luck dissipates, replaced by a newfound sense of control and fulfillment.

Good luck is not a random occurrence but a natural outcome of living in harmony with oneself. By healing the internal damage caused by covert bullying, individuals can restore the balance between their soul and psyche, unlocking the path to success, abundance, and meaningful relationships.

The covert bully targets need to recognize the impact it has had on their lives and take active steps toward healing and empowerment to break free from the debilitating effects of covert bullying.

BREAKING THE CYCLE AND RECLAIMING POTENTIAL

Therapeutic Intervention: Therapy, especially cognitive-behavioral therapy (CBT) and dialectical behavior therapy (DBT), is highly effective in helping targets process trauma, rebuild self-esteem, and develop healthier coping mechanisms. Addressing the psychological wounds caused by covert bullying is essential for overcoming the emotional barriers that block success.

Building Resilience: Developing resilience requires cultivating a strong sense of self-worth, setting healthy boundaries, and learning to counteract the manipulative tactics of covert bullies. By building resilience, targets can protect themselves from future manipulation and regain control over their lives and ambitions.

Fostering Financial Literacy and Independence: Learning financial management and gaining skills that enhance career prospects help targets regain financial stability and independence. Empowering targets to manage their finances is a key step in breaking free from the financial limitations imposed by covert bullying.

Reconnecting with Purpose and Passion: Encouraging targets to reconnect with their passions and purpose reignites their drive and motivation for success. Pursuing their true interests, whether through creative expression, entrepreneurship, or professional growth, can help targets overcome the energy blocks caused by covert bullying and unlock their full potential.

HEALING AND SUCCEEDING
AMID PSYCHOLOGICAL WARFARE

The journey to healing from covert bullying and gaslighting is not just about survival—it is about transformation, empowerment, and ultimately thriving. This journey, filled with opportunities for growth and self-discovery, leads to a brighter future. Covert bullying, with its subtle manipulation, creates deep wounds, leaving targets with distorted self-perceptions, feelings of isolation, and even physical health challenges. This chapter will walk individuals through reclaiming their power, profoundly healing, and finally achieving their full potential—emotionally, spiritually, personally, and financially.

Lifting the Veil of Shame: Reclaiming Power

Healing from covert bullying begins with the realization that there was never anything inherently wrong with the target. Their sensitivity, openness, and idealism made them vulnerable to emotional vampires, a term used to describe individuals who feed on the emotional energy of others. Shedding the burden of shame is the first step in recovery, enabling the target to analyze the calculated abuse for what it truly was. This awareness allows the target to see the bully as a weak individual who derives value and energy from exploiting others; unfortunately, the target was chosen merely to serve as a source of this emotional sustenance.

The hidden nature of familial covert bullying distorts the target's self-image, gradually eroding their confidence and inner compass. When targets try to speak up, they often do so without conviction and with feelings of shame, a shame compounded by society's tendency to stigmatize those who admit to being bullied. This societal response often adds a layer of difficulty, as targets may feel an added burden of humiliation simply for being targeted, leading them to question their own worth.

Covert bullying employs subtle tactics like veiled mockery (e.g., sarcastic comments disguised as jokes), gaslighting (e.g., causing the target to doubt their own memory or perception), and manipulation of societal norms (e.g., using societal expectations to control the target's behavior).

These tactics make it difficult for targets to confront or even recognize them as forms of abuse. Because society often shames those who are ridiculed, covert bullies gain a layer of protection, enabling them to perpetuate this damage while avoiding scrutiny. This societal response traps the target in a cycle of confusion and reinforces their isolation, making it even harder to break free from the cycle of abuse.

Reclaiming Power

Once the shame is lifted and the abuse is seen clearly, survivors can begin to reclaim their identity and inner strength. Recognizing the calculated nature of the attack allows them to break free from the cycle of self-doubt. With this newfound clarity, they can rebuild their self-worth, restore confidence, and pursue their true potential, all while practicing self-compassion and understanding that they are not to blame.

Challenging Self-Doubt and Shame

Covert bullying thrives on warping the target's perception of reality, leading to deep feelings of shame and self-doubt. Over time, the target may internalize false narratives, believing themselves to be weak or socially inept beliefs implanted by the abuser. Healing begins when targets acknowledge that these feelings of inadequacy are not personal failings but the result of deliberate psychological manipulation. By reclaiming their self-worth and validating their own experiences, targets take the first steps toward emotional clarity and autonomy.

The Sadness Phase: *A Necessary Step Toward Healing:*

One of the most common mistakes in the healing process is the desire to 'move on' quickly, bypassing the sadness phase. Proper recovery requires acknowledging the depth of harm inflicted. Targets need to grieve the loss of their sense of self actively, the humiliation they endured, and the opportunities and dreams stolen by covert bullying. It's crucial to recognize and honor this stage as a part of the healing journey, and it's equally important not to rush through it. Patience and understanding of one's own healing process are key. Moving beyond this phase empowers targets to reclaim their strength and progress toward genuine recovery.

The Role of Grief

The Role of Grief is central to this process. Grieving helps targets process emotional pain, opening the door to new growth and transformation. This sadness is a natural and valid part of healing; it deserves acknowledgment but is not meant as a permanent state. While there is no fixed timeline for grief, allowing oneself to experience it fully provides the strength to move forward. This balanced approach empowers targets to reclaim their strength, moving past the sadness toward genuine healing, which involves a deep understanding and acceptance of the past, and self-restoration, which is about rebuilding a positive sense of self and future.

Recognizing Patterns

By identifying these tactics, targets gain the power to protect themselves from future harm, allowing them to set firm boundaries and break free from the cycle of manipulation.

Understanding the Nature of the Covert Bully

Survivors must understand the covert bully's true nature to heal fully. Covert bullies are not simply misguided individuals—they are emotional 'vampires' who feed off their target's energy and well-being. Like vampires who drain their targets of blood, emotional vampires drain their targets of emotional energy, leaving them feeling depleted and exhausted. Their manipulation is deliberate and designed to erode the target's sense of self. These bullies thrive on emotional depletion and rarely change.

Targets of covert bullying are often chosen because their vulnerability or idealism makes them particularly susceptible to emotional manipulation. Many of these individuals may have encountered similar toxic figures earlier in life, and without healing, they are likely to attract these emotional vampires repeatedly.

Religious Context

Religious teachings acknowledge the potential for enmity within one's own family. For example:

Allah says:

"O you who have believed, indeed, among your spouses and your children are enemies to you, so beware of them." [Surah At-Taghabun: 14-18]

Similarly, in the Bible, Matthew 10:36 states:

"A man's enemies will be the members of his own household."

These verses underscore that covert bullies, much like emotional vampires, thrive when they find a suitable target, as change is not inherent to their nature.

Transmute Anger into Understanding

When confronting intense emotions, it is essential to work toward transforming anger into understanding. This shift in perspective enables stepping back from the emotional turmoil to gain insight into the underlying causes of the distress. By examining the dynamics at play, the impact of bullying can be unraveled, loosening anger's grip and paving the way for a deeper understanding of emotions. This process of clarity serves as a foundation for profound healing and emotional release, fostering a sense of control over feelings and overall well-being.

When emotions are embraced and understood, rage can be transformed into a catalyst for growth rather than a limiting force. This transformation fosters emotional freedom and opens the door to profound healing and personal empowerment, creating opportunities for self-discovery, strength, hope, and optimism.

Embrace the Complexity
of Emotions

Anger is a natural and reaction to covert bullying that damages self-respect, social connections, income, or quality of life. It's important to allow this anger to be fully experienced without self-judgment. Feelings of frustration and hurt reflect the depth of the harm and the seriousness of the wrongs suffered. While these emotions are valid, they don't define the end of the journey. Instead, they represent a necessary phase on the path toward healing and personal transformation.

Trust Your Intuition

Covert bullying erodes trust in one's instincts, leaving targets in a state of self-doubt. Reconnecting with intuition is a critical part of the healing journey. By creating space for introspection and minimizing distractions, targets can begin to unravel the layers of emotional manipulation.

Reclaiming Autonomy

Reclaiming autonomy is essential to healing. Covert bullies leave targets questioning their abilities and decisions. Survivors must rebuild trust in their instincts, set firm boundaries, and assert their personal needs to regain control.

Rebuilding Trust

Over time, targets can learn to trust their inner wisdom, using it to make decisions with greater clarity and confidence. This sense of intuition, nurtured through introspection and self-awareness, guides their path to self-assurance and personal growth.

Preventing Future Exploitation

Separating from the false beliefs imposed by the abuser is vital to reclaiming the target's true identity. Recognizing that covert bullies rarely change allows the target to prioritize emotional well-being and protect themselves from future manipulation.

CONFRONTING THE MENTAL
AND PHYSICAL HEALTH IMPACT
A HOLISTIC HEALING APPROACH

The emotional and physical toll of covert bullying is significant, causing anxiety, depression, chronic stress, and social withdrawal. These emotional wounds often manifest physically, leading to headaches, digestive issues, sleep disturbances, and a weakened immune system.

Emotional Recovery: Therapy is not just a tool for processing trauma; it's a path to peace. Mindfulness practices, like meditation and yoga, are not just stress relievers but gateways to mental clarity. As the target engages in these practices, each step becomes a step toward a brighter, more hopeful future.

Physical Recovery: Regular exercise, balanced nutrition, and proper sleep routines are crucial to restoring physical well-being.

OVERCOMING PROCRASTINATION

Breaking free from procrastination caused by covert bullying begins with recognizing its profound and pervasive impact. Procrastination is often rooted in a distorted sense of self-worth, shaped by the toxic narratives imposed by the bully—narratives that were never indeed one's own. This internalized self-doubt, a learned response rather than an inherent flaw, perpetuates avoidance, hesitation, and fear of failure.

This anxious desperation creates an energy of frustration and despair, trapping targets in a cycle of self-doubt. The constant hesitation repels opportunities, people, and success, further deepening feelings of inadequacy. Recovery requires a deliberate effort to address these psychological wounds, rebuild confidence, and develop self-resilience.

Recognizing the Damage: The first step is acknowledging the paralysis caused by covert bullying and understanding how it has taken hold. Procrastination is a learned response rooted in the bully's attempts to undermine confidence. Recognizing this connection is transformative, untangling the roots of inaction and paving the way for healing and action. Targets must confront the false comfort of "tomorrow" and begin taking deliberate, incremental steps today. No matter how small or imperfect, each action is a step out of the quicksand of procrastination, reclaiming potential and moving closer to a fulfilling life.

Cultivating Inner Peace: When individuals try to overcome procrastination, they often resort to excessive busyness as a way to feel productive. However, the solution lies in replacing this busyness, which merely aims to fill time, with work focused on achieving clear and specific goals. Working for the sake of working, or based on the false belief that being busy alone will solve problems, is not the right path. Every effort must be directed toward a defined purpose that contributes to genuine progress.

Purposeful and directed work, combined with cultivating inner peace, patience, and focus, is the key to breaking free from the shackles of self-doubt and avoiding the trap of meaningless busyness. Liberation from deeply ingrained resistance patterns requires a conscious and organized approach. Instead of waiting for the "perfect moment," which may never come, one must take proactive and effective steps toward meaningful goals that lead to real achievements.

A Structured Path Forward: Breaking free requires a structured approach to reprograming ingrained patterns of resistance. Like soldiers following orders, targets must act consistently without waiting for the "right time"—a moment that will never come. The path involves:

> Cultivating awareness of procrastination's roots.
>
> Taking small, consistent actions.
>
> Seeking guidance from trusted individuals or professionals.
>
> Practicing self-compassion and self-esteem-building activities.

Progress may feel slow, but consistency is critical. Even in uncertainty, action is the only way to escape the cycle of inaction. Each step forward helps reclaim time, dreams, and life itself, breaking the psychological chains of procrastination and self-doubt.

Challenging Perfectionism: To move forward, targets must confront the perfectionism that keeps them in a cycle of chasing unattainable ideals. Progress, not perfection, must become the goal. Accepting mistakes as a natural part of growth reduces the fear of failure and encourages small, steady actions.

Embracing Imperfection: Shifting from a perfectionist mindset to one that values progress is transformative.

Imperfections are not failures but opportunities for growth and learning. Adopting this perspective dissolves the paralyzing fear that holds targets back, opening the door to a brighter, more hopeful future.

Building Confidence Through Small Wins: Confidence grows through action. Starting with small, achievable goals helps reinforce belief in one's abilities. Each success builds momentum, gradually breaking the grip of procrastination and self-doubt.

Setting Boundaries and Developing Resilience: Establishing boundaries is essential to prevent further harm. Resilience develops as targets learn to handle criticism and setbacks without internalizing them. Practicing self-compassion counters the negative self-talk instilled by the bully, fostering emotional strength and a foundation for growth.

Overcoming the Brain's Resistance to Change
Scientific and Spiritual Perspectives

One of the most significant challenges in healing from covert bullying is overcoming the brain's resistance to healing. This resistance is rooted in both science and spirituality.

Scientific Perspective: The brain is designed for survival, often clinging to familiar patterns, even when harmful. Trauma causes the brain to focus on safety rather than growth, reinforcing negative beliefs and behaviors through established neural pathways. While neuroplasticity, the brain's capacity to form new connections, is critical to healing, overcoming these ingrained patterns demands intentional effort to rewire the brain.

Spiritual Perspective: Spiritually, this resistance stems from the ego's fear of transformation. The ego clings to familiar identities, even those formed through targethood. Healing requires facing the discomfort of letting go and trusting in the unknown.

Ego's Fear of Transformation

Overcoming Resistance

Through mindfulness, therapy, and spiritual practices, the target can reprogram their mind and embrace change. By confronting the brain's resistance and trusting in the healing process, the target can break free from the past and create a healthier, more empowered future.

Rebuilding Personality and Establishing

Strong Boundaries: Covert bullying profoundly affects the target's personality, leaving lasting scars that distort their sense of self and erode confidence. As a result, targets often struggle with social cues, lack assertiveness, and may even experience diminished attractiveness due to a loss of self-esteem and emotional well-being. Rebuilding personality is a crucial aspect of the healing process and involves deep introspection and setting firm boundaries to protect emotional health.

Self-Discovery

Targets must reflect on how covert abuse shaped their personalities and stifled their growth. Covert bullies undermine their targets by subtly manipulating their emotions, which often 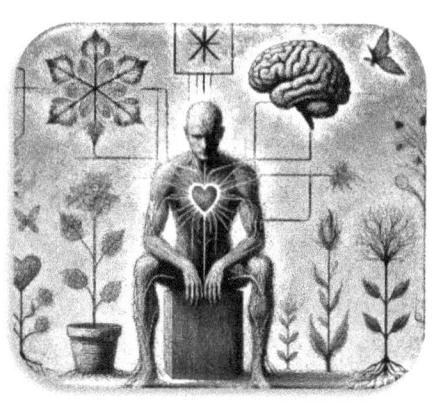 leaves targets questioning their social skills and self-worth. Many internalize the abuse, leading to feelings of inadequacy and confusion in social situations. This process can cause them to miss or misinterpret social cues, making interactions challenging and contributing to feelings of isolation.

Reclaiming their identity is essential for developing resilience, self-worth, and social confidence. As targets rediscover their authentic selves, they can begin to correct how the abuse distorted their behavior and social understanding. Rebuilding this identity helps them re-engage with the world on their terms, cultivating more genuine connections with others.

Setting Boundaries and Cutting Ties with Toxic Influences

Setting Boundaries: Establishing firm boundaries is not just a part of rebuilding; it's a shield of protection. Covert bullies often exploit a lack of clear boundaries to manipulate their targets, eroding the target's sense of control. Learning to set and maintain these boundaries is crucial for emotional protection and healing. As the target sets these boundaries, they are not just rebuilding self-confidence but enhancing their social attractiveness by asserting their right to be treated with respect and dignity.

Cutting Ties with Toxic Influences: A Solo Journey

Reclaiming power involves cutting ties with toxic influences—the covert bully and those who enable or reinforce harmful behaviors. This process is about protecting the target's emotional well-being and embracing solitude as a powerful tool for healing.

Steps to Cutting Ties:

Acknowledging the Harm: Identifying relationships that contribute to emotional distress and imbalance.

Setting Boundaries: Establishing emotional distance by defining and maintaining clear personal limits.

Limiting Communication: Gradually reducing interaction and avoiding conversations that drain emotional energy.

Cutting Ties: Ending communication entirely when a relationship begins to negatively affect well-being.

The Power of Forgiveness

A Path to Liberation and Personal Growth

Embrace Forgiveness as a Path to Liberation

Forgiveness, particularly after enduring covert bullying, is often misunderstood as condoning or excusing the abuser's behavior. However, true forgiveness is not about absolving the perpetrator of their harmful actions. Instead, it is a profound act of

self-liberation, allowing the target to release the emotional chains that tie them to the trauma. By choosing to forgive, the target takes a deliberate step toward reclaiming their emotional and psychological freedom.

The Process of Forgiveness: Forgiveness is not an overnight transformation or a linear process. It requires patience, self-compassion, and multiple stages of reflection and emotional release. The target must first confront the depth of the hurt and acknowledge the full impact of the abuse. This may involve grieving for the lost sense of self, missed opportunities, or the emotional toll the bullying took.

Once the target has processed these emotions, they can release the attachment to the trauma. This step is crucial because forgiveness is not about justifying the bully's actions but about breaking those actions' hold onto the target's psyche. By mentally and emotionally distancing themselves from the covert abuser's behavior, the target can begin to untangle their sense of self from the narrative imposed by the bully.

Reclaiming Personal Power: One of the most profound outcomes of forgiveness is the reclamation of personal power. By choosing to forgive, targets no longer allow their abusers to control their emotions or thoughts. They reclaim their ability to dictate how they feel and what they value. Forgiveness restores a sense of agency, allowing individuals to see themselves as more than just a product of their trauma.

This newfound power manifests in various ways. Emotionally, targets feel lighter as resentment no longer consumes their energy. Mentally, they gain clarity as memories of the abuse no longer dominate their thoughts. Spiritually, forgiveness can lead to a more profound sense of peace and connection with oneself, as it signals a return to the target's authentic self, un-burdened by the toxic influence of the bully.

Forgiveness as a Path to Growth: Beyond the immediate relief it provides, forgiveness is also a powerful catalyst for personal growth. In letting go of the past, targets create space for new experiences, relationships, and opportunities. They are no longer stuck in a cycle of rehashing old wounds but are free to move forward with their lives with a renewed sense of purpose and direction.

Forgiveness allows individuals to embrace the lessons learned from their bullying experience. They emerge from the process stronger, with a deeper understanding of their resilience and healing ability. By transforming the pain of the past into wisdom, targets are better equipped to navigate future challenges with grace and confidence.

Self-Forgiveness

A vital yet often overlooked part of forgiveness is self-forgiveness. Targets of covert bullying frequently carry feelings of guilt or shame,

mistakenly believing they somehow allowed the abuse or should have recognized the signs sooner. However, self-forgiveness is just as crucial as forgiving the abuser. It requires acknowledging that the target is not responsible for the bully's actions and understanding that their vulnerability, openness, or trust was never a flaw but a strength that was unfairly exploited. Without awareness of the darker sides of human nature, this trait may come across as naïve in society.

By embracing self-forgiveness, individuals release the burden of self-blame, opening the door to a more compassionate and empowering relationship with themselves. This process allows them to view their past not through a lens of regret but with a sense of growth and resilience.

The Liberation of Forgiveness: Ultimately, forgiveness is a path to liberation. It frees the target from the toxic emotional ties that bind them to the past, allowing them to step into a future unencumbered by pain, anger, or resentment. In this liberated state, individuals can fully reclaim their power, live authentically, and embrace the possibilities that lie ahead. Forgiveness is not a gift to the bully but to oneself, a way of honoring one's strength, worth, and capacity to heal. Through forgiveness, targets of covert bullying find the freedom to move beyond their trauma and reclaim their lives with dignity, grace, and self-empowerment.

THE POWER OF SILENCE IN HEALING:

WHY HEALING IS A SOLO JOURNEY

THE POWER OF SOLITUDE IN HEALING

The Pitfall of Over-Talking: When emotionally distressed, the instinct to seek comfort through excessive talking can intensify the chaos rather than calm it. Rehashing painful details may reinforce the emotional turmoil, pulling the target deeper into the past rather than moving toward peace. Additionally, well-meaning friends or family might offer unhelpful advice or diminish the significance of feelings, further complicating recovery.

Silence as a Path to Inner Clarity: Healing begins when the target embraces silence. When they stop seeking external validation, they create a sacred space to process emotions meaningfully and privately. Silence allows them to connect with their inner wisdom, listen to their feelings, and gain clarity from quiet reflection. Silence provides the necessary calm to confront difficult emotions, work through inner conflicts, and rediscover inner strength.

Healing is a Solo Journey: No one can fully understand the depth of the target's pain or guide them through healing better than themselves. Healing is a solo journey that must be navigated independently. Though sharing experiences may seem comforting, true healing comes from introspection, not external validation. Professional support from therapists is helpful, but the real transformation happens within the target during moments of solitude.

Embrace Solitude

A Path to Inner Growth and Creativity

Solitude is not a void, but a powerful space for personal growth and reinvention. It's a time when you can rediscover your true self, free from external pressures and harmful influences. This period of isolation is an opportunity for deep reflection, allowing you to explore who you are outside the shadow of toxic dynamics. It's a chance to rebuild your identity, strengthen your emotional resilience and lay the foundation for a more, empowered, self-assured version of yourself. Instead of viewing solitude as loneliness, consider it a time for healing and rediscovery. It's a time to regain clarity, purpose, and inner strength. Silence becomes a companion supporting your inward journey, helping you reflect on your experiences and emerge stronger, with a clearer understanding of your path to healing.

The Importance of Solitude in Healing

Solitude is an essential tool in recovery, allowing the target to reconnect with themselves without external pressure. In this quiet space, they can reassess what truly matters, rediscover their values, and rebuild emotional strength. Through solitude, the target transforms isolation into empowerment, setting the stage for continued personal growth and emotional freedom.

Physical and Emotional Clutter & Chaos

Decluttering as a Form of Emotional Release

Decluttering is more than just tidying up physical spaces; it's a powerful act of emotional release. When a target consciously lets go of unnecessary items—whether an old gift from a toxic relationship, items tied to painful memories, or outdated clothing that no longer aligns with who they are—they're not just clearing out physical space but making room for emotional healing.

These objects often carry emotional weight, and by releasing them, the target begins to process and release the emotions tied to them. This act of decluttering serves as a form of closure, allowing the target to unburden themselves from the past and make space for new beginnings.

The Link Between Physical Clutter and Emotional Chaos

Physical clutter has a profound impact on mental and emotional states. Studies show that a disorganized environment can increase stress levels, reduce focus, and even contribute to anxiety or depression. For targets of covert bullying or emotional manipulation, clutter can symbolize the emotional weight they carry. Every item in their space may reflect unresolved issues or unprocessed emotions, keeping them tethered to the past and hindering personal growth.

Creating a Space for Peace and Clarity

Removing physical clutter creates an open space that fosters peace and clarity. A clean and organized space promotes a calm mind, allowing the target to focus on the present moment and make informed decisions for their future. In a decluttered environment, the target feels more in control and empowered, with newfound mental energy to direct toward self-reflection, creativity, and emotional well-being. This newly created space becomes a blank canvas for positive energy and personal growth.

Decluttering the Mind

Just as physical spaces accumulate clutter, so too does the mind. Mental clutter consists of unhelpful thoughts, worries, and unresolved emotional baggage that cloud thinking and weigh the target emotionally. For example, constant rumination on past events or negative self-perceptions can prevent progress and healing. To declutter their mind, the target must cultivate self-awareness, identify these harmful thought patterns, and release them to create space for inner peace and emotional clarity.

Decluttering is not a one-time task but an ongoing process that requires intention, effort, and self-awareness. The target should start small, focusing on one area of their home or category of thoughts at a time. With each step, they create a ripple effect of clarity and peace in both their physical and mental environments. This decluttering process aligns with deeper self-discovery and healing, allowing the target to release what no longer serves them and create room for new opportunities, a healthier mindset, and personal growth.

Conclusion: Emotional Freedom Through Decluttering

In conclusion, decluttering is not just about tidying up; it's an essential step toward emotional freedom and self-healing. As the target lets go of what no longer serves them, they create space for clarity, peace, and personal transformation. The target lays the foundation for a more fulfilling, empowered, and growth-oriented life by crafting a space that reflects their true self and core values.

ESCAPING ENVY AND TOXIC COMPETITION

THE PATH TO TRUE SUCCESS

THE PIT OF UNCONSCIOUS COMPETITION

While jealousy is an Inherent feeling all humans possess, it can be dormant for targets of covert bullying. After waking up to the reality of clandestine abuse, which often brings jealousy to the surface, especially after realizing how much time and energy the bully has drained, it is natural to feel hatred, anger, and envy toward the bully and others who appear to have had an easier path is natural.

Unconscious Jealousy can quickly transform into burning envy, leading to dangerous consequences. However, with self-awareness, Jealousy can be harnessed as a tool for success. This self-awareness highlights areas that need improvement while emphasizing qualities that should be accepted and embraced with pride, such as physical features. It empowers you to take control of your emotions and use them for personal growth.

Jealousy vs Envy

Understanding the difference between envy and jealousy is enlightening and empowering. Where jealousy is a natural, stagnant emotion, envy lingers. Envy drives one into perpetual comparison, dissatisfaction, toxic competition, Schadenfreude, and criminal activities. By grasping this difference, we gain a powerful tool to put ourselves in the driver's seat of our vice emotional journey. Covert bullies plant seeds of doubt and inferiority, and even after breaking free, the anger to make up for lost time can be a trap for proving one's worth through competition and obsessive thoughts of revenge. This path of envy only leads to insecurity and self-doubt, continuing the cycle of emotional abuse, but now it is oneself.

Navigating Jealousy in a Healthy Way

Jealousy Without Judgment: It is crucial to acknowledge jealousy as a natural human emotion without judgment or shame, make peace with it, and allow it to pass. Recognizing jealousy helps prevent it from taking control, providing insight into what it reveals, before letting it go without acting on it.

Focus Inward: Shifting focus from others to personal growth. Jealousy is not an emotion to be ashamed of; it can serve as a guiding emotion that highlights areas where growth is needed. Rather than viewing it negatively, it can be seen as an opportunity for self-improvement, ultimately leading to success in all areas.

Prioritize Progress, Not Competition: Toxic competition can be avoided by focusing on personal milestones rather than comparing them to others. Each individual's life journey is unique.

Cultivate Gratitude and Self-Compassion: Acknowledging every small achievement and practicing self-compassion helps prevent envy and keeps individuals grounded in their personal progress.

Channel Jealousy Positively: Redirecting jealousy into positive growth involves setting small steps to achieve goals, rather than allowing competition to drive the journey.

Avoid Feeding the Ego: Envy often arises from a need for external validation and self-doubt. Resisting the urge to prove oneself reduces ego-driven actions, allowing healing and growth to take priority, even when envy provides only a temporary sense of satisfaction.

Toxic Competition

Toxic competition creates barriers to success, such as constantly comparing one's achievements to those of others, feeling resentful when others succeed, or engaging in Schadenfeude. Energy is Squandered when the focus shifts from achieving personal goals to outdoing others. Instead of investing in growth and improvement, comparison and resentment take over.

True success comes from personal alignment with values and fulfillment, which means achieving goals that align with your beliefs and bring you a sense of satisfaction. But toxic competition clouds this process. Focusing on others' progress instead of one's own causes anxiety, frustration, and unhappiness. Constantly trying to outdo others prevents noticing opportunities for creativity and personal growth.

Achieving Success Through Personal Growth

Progress must be measured against one's past self rather than others. Focusing on self-improvement instead of unconscious competition is essential to success and contentment. Personal growth can be achieved through mindfulness, praying, self-reflection, setting and achieving personal goals. It clears the emotional pain caused by envy and comparison.

Letting go of envy is not easy; it is a liberation through self-resistance. It frees individuals to pursue what truly matters without chasing a mirage that leads them to the pit of hell. This release from the burden of envy brings a profound sense of relief and lightness, allowing you to focus on personal growth and fulfillment, feeling liberated and concentrating on your journey.

Focusing on personal growth clears the path to success, free from envy's distractions. Energy previously wasted on rivalry becomes available to build something meaningful and aligned with individual purpose. This mindset shift opens doors to new opportunities, creativity, and long-term success, where achievements result from hard work, not others' failures. Focusing on personal growth is not just a strategy; it's a source of empowerment and confidence, making you feel more self-assured and in control of your journey.

Embrace Self-Acceptance and Healing

Healing from covert bullying is grounded in self-acceptance, inner peace, and personal triumph. It's essential to embrace all emotions, including jealousy, without judgment or allowing them to dominate. By acknowledging and sitting with negative feelings, they can pass with self-awareness, paving the way for growth beyond the destructive patterns of envy. This process empowers and strengthens resilience.

Instead of fueling envy, the focus shifts to empowerment, with lessons from the past building resilience and strength. Healing is not about surpassing others but becoming the best version of oneself, free from the toxicity of comparison and competition. Practicing self-affirmation, praying, setting personal goals, and celebrating small victories builds a strong sense of self-worth that isn't dependent on external opinions. By embracing this journey, the key to success becomes evident. The soundest victories come from inner peace, self-awareness, and personal growth—not from competition or validation from others.

CONSCIOUS REVENGE
A HEALING TACTIC
(WITHOUT FALLING INTO TOXIC REVENGE)

One of the most unconventional yet empowering healing tactics is conscious revenge. Rather than engaging in destructive retaliation, it focuses on mindfully reclaiming personal power. By transforming the pain and injustice inflicted by others, conscious revenge becomes a powerful tool for personal growth, success, and empowerment.

In situations of covert bullying or toxic influences, the target often feels powerless and emotionally drained. Conscious revenge shifts the focus from targethood to agency, allowing you to use the desire for justice to heal and thrive. While this approach empowers healing, it's essential to distinguish conscious revenge from toxic revenge rooted in anger and bitterness.

Conscious revenge is about reclaiming control of your life, emotions, and future by focusing on your success and well-being, not on getting even. Toxic revenge is driven by anger and the desire to inflict pain. Conscious revenge redirects that energy into self-improvement, lifting you above the harm caused.

How Does Conscious Revenge Work

Channeling Energy into Personal Success: Channeling Energy into Personal Success Instead of harboring resentment or seeking to harm those who have caused harm, conscious revenge focuses on channeling that energy into personal achievement. Redirecting efforts toward goals in areas such as career, relationships, or self-development transforms negative energy into a powerful force for success. The true power of 'revenge' lies in demonstrating the ability to rise above the harm inflicted, turning pain into progress.

Reclaiming Power Through Self-Worth: Covert bullies often undermine their targets' self-worth. Conscious revenge is about rebuilding self-esteem. It involves refusing to let others' negative actions define your value and choosing to see yourself as worthy, despite adversity.

Setting and Enforcing Boundaries: Setting clear, firm boundaries with those who have caused harm actively protects energy and mental well-being. This decisive action refuses to tolerate toxic behavior and sends a powerful message that poor treatment is no longer accepted.

Silent Triumph

It is crucial to understand that people often hold preconceived notions about the target's level of success. These preconceived ideas, shaped by past experiences or biases, are difficult to change. When others cling to such fixed perceptions, they create an energetic barrier that subtly affects the target, draining focus and potentially hindering the ability to align energetically, resulting in delays or obstacles to success.

Merely sharing details about progress can give others opportunities for negative interference—whether through energetic disruption (such as constant criticism or undermining comments) or direct actions by the covert bully (like spreading rumors or sabotaging work)—which could derail success entirely.

By remaining silent and moving forward quietly, the target deprives others of the satisfaction of knowing the next steps, leaving them under the illusion that they have succeeded in undermining confidence. This silence becomes the greatest ally, as it protects against further sabotage and allows the target to focus fully on steadily building success, free from external interference and risks. Refusing to engage ensures that progress is made away from the reach of negative influence, enabling success to develop smoothly and quietly.

Staying on the Path of Conscious Revenge

Redirecting energy toward personal goals instead of seeking the downfall of others transforms toxic revenge into conscious growth. Channeling effort into building a fulfilling life diminishes the grip of past pain, turning success into the ultimate silent victory.

Transforming Pain into Personal Development: The hurt and betrayal experienced can serve as motivation for growth. Investing in self-improvement—such as learning new skills, building resilience, and enhancing overall well-being—turns adversity into a catalyst for success. Thriving despite harm becomes the ultimate measure of triumph.

Cultivating Inner Peace: Conscious revenge focuses on achieving peace and fulfillment rather than keeping score. Toxic revenge traps individuals in the cycle of reliving past grievances, while cultivating inner peace through mindfulness, gratitude, and emotional balance promotes true liberation and growth.

Establishing Boundaries: Instead of Seeking Retaliation Rather than retaliating against those who caused harm, conscious revenge emphasizes creating healthy boundaries. Protecting well-being through distancing from toxic individuals ensures progress and emotional safety, without resorting to harmful actions.

Measuring Success by Personal Growth, *Not Others' Failure*: Toxic revenge measures success by the suffering of others, but conscious revenge focuses on personal growth. The journey is defined by progress and resilience, regardless of whether those who caused harm acknowledge their actions or their impact.

Forgiveness as a Path to Freedom: Forgiveness plays a vital role in conscious revenge—not to absolve the wrongdoer, but to achieve inner peace. Letting go of bitterness releases emotional burdens and severs the toxic grip of the past. This act is not about excusing harm but about reclaiming emotional and mental freedom.

Conscious Revenge as a Healing Mechanism: This approach channels the desire for justice into a constructive force for healing and growth. Rather than being consumed by anger or the urge for retaliation, conscious revenge emphasizes self-improvement and transformation. It reclaims power by using difficult experiences as fuel for progress, turning pain into strength.

Conscious revenge ultimately serves as a testament to resilience, proving that challenges can be transformed into opportunities for growth. It is about quietly demonstrating strength and using success as a powerful statement of overcoming adversity.

THE POWER OF STAYING STILL

EMBRACING DISCOMFORT TO BREAK THE CYCLE OF ANXIETY

For targets of covert bullying, the emotional toll of constant manipulation and undermining can lead to heightened restlessness and anxiety. Over time, they develop a deep-seated fear of discomfort and an overwhelming urge to escape emotional pain. As a result, even minor challenges can feel like insurmountable burdens, pushing them to the edge and triggering thoughts like, "Here's another thing to give me more anxiety.

When targets receive minor criticism, for example, instead of viewing it as constructive feedback, their mind spirals into anxiety with thoughts like, "What if I'm not good enough?" or "This person is out to destroy me," or "This is another example of my failure." They become consumed with worry, believing that this minor incident confirms their worst fears and insecurities, leading to emotional distress disproportionate to the event. In these situations, the instinct is often to react immediately—by attacking the source, engaging in self-attack, or avoiding the discomfort altogether.

They miss opportunities, which further deepens their anxiety—an anxiety that can only be relieved by facing and overcoming challenges. This cycle continues because they haven't learned how to tolerate uncomfortable emotions and allow them to pass. Their automatic response is to escape or overreact because they associate feeling bad with something fundamentally wrong with themselves or their lives. Breaking this cycle requires learning the power of staying still sitting with discomfort even when the urge to escape feels overwhelming. And that doesn't mean suppressing emotions or pretending the pain isn't there. Instead, it's about acknowledging and accepting the pain, allowing it to run its course without impulsive reactions.

By staying still in moments of discomfort, individuals realize that pain is temporary and doesn't always require immediate action or full-on self-attack, giving them more control over their emotional reactions. As they build emotional resilience, targets of covert bullying come to understand that not every stressor is a catastrophe. They learn that while discomfort or pain may be intense, it is temporary, and they have the strength to endure it. This realization is crucial for those conditioned to believe they are powerless in the face of discomfort, reinforcing the belief that pain is always wrong and must be avoided at all costs.

For instance, instead of reacting to a friend not immediately responding to a message as if it's a life-or-death situation, they can practice sitting with the initial anxiety. Over time, they'll recognize that the discomfort will pass without acting on every fear or insecurity. By developing emotional strength to tolerate discomfort without reacting impulsively, targets of covert bullying can regain control over their emotional state. They learn to make peace with uncomfortable feelings, recognizing that resisting pain only amplifies it. By allowing pain to arise, pass, and even gain insight from it, they can break the cycle of anxiety, and that may lead to relief and a deeper understanding that pain doesn't have to define one's actions or self-worth. Through this practice, they navigate life's challenges with greater calm and clarity, learning to ride the wave of discomfort rather than being overwhelmed by it.

THE POWER OF SETTING GOALS
WEIGHING PAIN AGAINST PURPOSE

Life is a constant balancing act, a scale upon which we weigh the pain of the present against the joy of achieving our goals. Mental strength is the key to navigating this scale. It's about deciding, every day, which side of the scale will carry more weight: the temporary discomfort of effort or the long-term fulfillment of success. Those who succeed understand that pain is inevitable but also fleeting. the joy of achieving a meaningful goal, however, lasts a lifetime.

Mental strength isn't just about enduring hardships, it's about perspective. It's the ability to zoom out and see beyond the immediate struggle. When the pain of effort feels overwhelming, it's easy to focus on how complex the journey is. But those with mental resilience know how to focus on the bigger picture. They visualize the joy, pride, and sense of accomplishment waiting at the finish line, and they use that vision to tip the scale in favor of persistence.

This scale applies to every choice we make. Do we let the weight of our pain stop us from climbing higher, or do we recognize that enduring this moment is the price of success? Those who focus only on the weight of their struggles risk staying stagnant, trapped in a cycle of excuses and regrets. But those who choose to bear the burden of effort understand that it lightens with time while the rewards grow heavier and more significant.

Even religious teachings highlight this principle. Striving for meaningful, virtuous goals often requires sacrifice, discipline, and self-restraint. Yet the rewards, whether personal growth, spiritual fulfillment, or achieving something genuinely remarkable—should always outweigh the cost required to achieve it. The scale eventually tips in favor of those who choose to bear the burden of effort. The heavy weight of consequences for those who seek shortcuts, choosing unethical or easy paths, replaces the temporary relief they sought. This reassures us that the ethical path, though challenging, yields lasting rewards.

Mental strength consistently tipping the scale in favor of long-term joy over short-term comfort. It's about understanding that achieving authentic, legal, and morally sound goals is the hardest thing we can do and the most rewarding. Each time we face a choice, we are shaping our future.

The stronger we become mentally, the more equipped we are to face the pain of effort and turn it into the foundation of our success. This empowerment gives us control over our future, making us the architects of our own success. In the end, success isn't just about reaching the goal. It's about proving to yourself that you were strong enough to tip the scales in your favor time and time again until you build a life of purpose and pride. This journey of success, filled with challenges and triumphs, should inspire and motivate us to keep tipping the scales in our favor.

THE EMOTIONAL AND SPIRITUAL DRIVE
OF
RESPONSIBILITY
A PATH TO SUCCESS

Responsibility, a potent catalyst for success, possesses a transformative power that can infuse life with profound meaning and propel individuals to greatness. The emotional connection to responsibility, especially when it involves loved ones, has the potential to revolutionize a person's perspective and ignite their determination. Goals become more compelling and achievable when tied to an emotional purpose, as the human brain thrives on these connections.

Children embody this principle. They are not just responsibilities but also blessings that bring emotional and spiritual prosperity. Across various religious traditions, children are seen as bearers of good fortune. In Islam, for example, children are regarded as blessings from Allah, with the Quran highlighting their role as both a test and a reward. This verse reflects the dual nature of children as both a responsibility and a source of prosperity, not through miraculous wealth but through the emotional and motivational transformation they inspire in parents.

Similarly, in Hinduism, children are seen as bearers of good fortune. Their births are celebrated with rituals, reflecting the belief that they bring prosperity and ensure the family's stability. The concept of Putra (son) traditionally highlights the importance of children in carrying forward the family lineage and economic well-being. Even in Christianity, while children are primarily viewed as spiritual blessings, larger families historically contributed to economic productivity in agricultural societies, where more children meant more hands to work the land.

This universal recognition of children as blessings underscores a fundamental truth: their presence anchors individuals to goals more significant than themselves. In Islam, the idea of children bringing blessings is not about divine miracles raining wealth from the heavens but about the emotional transformation that responsibility brings. Parents often discover new levels of patience, resilience, and motivation, using these qualities to overcome challenges and achieve success.

The "blessing" of children lies in their ability to create an emotional drive that outweighs present pain or struggle. Parents often find themselves persevering, not because the journey is easy, but because the responsibility of providing a better future for their children gives them purpose. This emotional drive becomes the fuel for personal growth, resilience, and discipline. It pushes individuals to become the best version of themselves, building a future that endures far beyond the current struggles. However, it's important to acknowledge that this journey is not without its challenges and sacrifices. It often demands discipline, sacrifice, and perseverance.

Moreover, having multiple children can amplify this effect. Each child serves as a reminder of purpose and legacy, reinforcing the stakes of one's efforts. Parents' sacrifices often feel less burdensome when weighed against the joy and fulfillment children bring. This constant emotional drive keeps parents focused and committed, turning challenges into steppingstones toward personal and family growth.

Success often requires a combination of emotional drive and the mental strength to weigh goals against pain. Responsibility, particularly to loved ones, provides the fire needed to tip the scale in favor of progress. Religious teachings universally emphasize the importance of striving for meaningful and virtuous goals, and children often serve as the emotional anchors that make this possible. Their presence often leads to a deeper spiritual growth, which in turn, fuels personal development and success. This spiritual growth can manifest in various ways, from a deepened sense of purpose to a stronger connection to one's community or faith.

While achieving these goals may demand discipline, sacrifice, and perseverance, the rewards far outweigh the costs. In this way, children are a blessing—not because they make life easier, but because they give life meaning. They inspire individuals to overcome adversity, achieve greatness, and leave a legacy of purpose and pride. Whether viewed through the lens of faith, culture, or personal growth, the emotional and spiritual drive children provide is a powerful force that propels us toward success.

TOUGHEN UP

Covert Bullying: The Silent Epidemic

Covert bullying within families is a silent epidemic, subtly weaving its destructive effects across cultures, societies, and generations. It often operates so quietly that its targets remain unaware until they are deeply entrenched in self-doubt. This epidemic plants seeds of limiting beliefs—those persistent whispers of *"You're not enough," "You can't succeed,"* or *"You don't deserve better."*

The outcomes are evident worldwide: big success is less common than no success. This disparity isn't due to a lack of talent or ambition. Instead, familial covert bullying lays a foundation of fear and inadequacy that many struggle to overcome. But the cycle can be broken. There comes a point in every journey when the Way forward demands a revolution—not against others, but within oneself. Familial covert bullying may have shaped how you see yourself and what you believe is possible, but transformation begins with **awareness**. By recognizing the patterns holding you back, you can raise a "coup on yourself," overthrowing the limiting beliefs and habits that no longer serve you.

Familial Covert Bullying: The Silent Saboteur

Familial covert bullying thrives on dynamics such as: Sabotage through Subtlety: Confidence is chipped away with backhanded compliments or dismissive remarks.

Inherited Limitation: Beliefs like *"People like us can't succeed"* are passed down, creating a mindset of mediocrity.

Fear-Based Conditioning: Fear of failure or rejection is used to stifle ambition.

Unspoken Expectations: Silent pressures to conform discourage individuality and boldness.

The Ripple Effect of Limiting Beliefs

Limiting beliefs are the invisible shackles created by covert bullying. They manifest as:

Settling for Mediocrity: Avoiding ambitious goals because they seem unattainable.

Fear of Failure: Being paralyzed by the possibility of rejection or setbacks.

Internal Conflict: Feeling unworthy of success, as though it would betray family or loved ones.

When unchallenged, these beliefs perpetuate cycles of underachievement—not just in individuals but across societies.

The Inner Coup

A Journey to Overthrow Limiting Beliefs

A coup on oneself isn't a single event; it's a continuous process of dismantling the old systems of doubt, guilt, and fear instilled by covert bullying. This inner revolution requires courage, discipline, and faith in your ability to build a new, empowering internal framework.

Steps to Overthrow the Old System

Awareness: Recognize the Patterns

Just as spiritual leaders call for reflection and repentance, your transformation begins with acknowledging how familial covert bullying has influenced your choices and beliefs. Awareness is your first act of rebellion against the constraints imposed on you.

Repent and Renew

Repentance in this context is about releasing false narratives. Let go of *"I'm not enough"* and replace it with affirmations of possibility and strength. Renew your sense of self-worth and potential.

Raise the Standards of Your Being

In Islam, the concept of *Tazkiyah* (purification of the soul) teaches that success lies in elevating oneself beyond distractions and mediocrity. Similarly, raise your internal standards— dream bigger, act bolder, and know that you were created for greatness.

Discipline: The Key to Lasting Change

Transformation demands consistent effort. The Bible reminds us:

"No discipline seems pleasant at the time, but painful. Later on, however, it produces a harvest of righteousness and peace" (Hebrews 12:11).

Faith and Action: Trust the Process

Religious teachings emphasize the harmony between faith and action. Trust in the Divine plan while taking deliberate steps to build the life you deserve. Remember:

"God does not change the condition of a people until they change what is in themselves" *(Quran 13:11).*

Religious and Spiritual Path to Transformation

Spiritual traditions across cultures provide frameworks for breaking free from mental prisons and stepping into personal liberation.

Hinduism: Liberation Through Self-Knowledge

Teaching: *"The mind is restless and hard to control, but it can be tamed through practice and detachment"* (*Bhagavad Gita* 6:35).

Practice: Meditation and self-inquiry dissolve ignorance and help transcend false identities.

Judaism: Renewal Through Teshuvah

Teaching: *"Do not say, 'When I free myself, I will study,' for perhaps you will never free yourself"* (*Pirkei Avot* 2:5).

Practice: Self-reflection and confession enable a return to authenticity and alignment with one's true self.

Buddhism: The Middle Path to Freedom

Teaching: *"What you think, you become. What you feel, you attract. What you imagine, you create"* (*Dhammapada* 1:1).

Practice: Mindfulness and meditation cultivate awareness and detachment, freeing the mind from suffering.

Christianity: Renewing the Mind

Teaching: *"Do not conform to the pattern of this world, but be transformed by the renewing of your mind"* (*Romans 12:2*).

Practice: Prayer and surrendering fears to God enable inner peace and spiritual growth.

Islam: Self-Purification and Trust in Allah

Teaching: *"Indeed, with hardship comes ease"* (*Quran 94:6*).

Practice: Prayers, fasting, and charity purify the heart and mind while fostering resilience and clarity.

Sufism: Breaking the Ego's Chains

Teaching: *"The soul that is free of ego is the soul that is closest to God"* (*Rumi*).

Practice: Reciting *dhikr* and meditative practices dissolve the ego's grip and liberate the mind.

Taoism: Aligning with the Flow

Teaching: *"When I let go of what I am, I become what I might be"* (*Tao Te Ching* 44).

Practice: Simplicity and non-resistance align individuals with the natural flow of life, fostering clarity.

Native American Spirituality: Harmony and Vision

Teaching: *"The longest journey you will make in your life is from your head to your heart.*

Practice: Vision quests and rituals in nature reconnect individuals with their inner truth, releasing societal limitations.

Modern Spirituality: Reprogramming the Subconscious

Teaching: *"Your subconscious mind is your servant. Whatever you plant in it will grow"* (*Joseph Murphy*).

Practice: Affirmations and visualization help rewrite internal narratives, breaking free from mental limitations.

Universal Teaching: Freedom From Oneself

Across traditions, a timeless wisdom emerges: *"Freedom begins with awareness, faith, and consistent action."* Through reflection, prayer, and dedicated practice, these teachings guide individuals to dissolve their inner mental prisons and unlock their fullest potential. This journey is both a spiritual awakening and a practical transformation, paving the way to a life of purpose, fulfillment, and success."

From Pain to Prosperity: Building a New System

Raising a Coup on Oneself

Breaking free from the effects of covert bullying involves more than just escaping its influence—it requires building an entirely new internal system grounded in:

Self-Worth: Recognizing inherent value and deservingness of success.

Financial Independence: Making empowered choices to secure a stable and prosperous future.

Spiritual Alignment: Living in accordance with one's highest values and purpose.

This transformation represents both a spiritual awakening and a practical revolution.

Redefining Loyalty

Loyalty transcends conformity to restrictive family dynamics. It entails breaking the cycle of covert bullying to establish a legacy of strength, resilience, and abundance for future generations.

Strengthening and Overcoming

Awareness is the first tool in dismantling the impact of familial covert bullying. This process involves:

Confronting Conditioning: Questioning inherited beliefs and identifying the origins of limiting internal narratives.

Replacing Fear with Action: Each bold step diminishes the grip of fear and restrictive conditioning.

Embracing a New Narrative: Rewriting the story to reflect boundless potential and capability.

Becoming the Exception

Exceptional success is rare because few dare to challenge ingrained psychological systems. True strength lies not in suppressing emotions but in refining one's spirit and sharpening focus to rise above.

This is the moment to transcend limitations and achieve greatness—not only for personal fulfillment but as a beacon of inspiration for the world. Success is waiting to be claimed.

GRATITUDE THROUGH HEALING AMID FAMILIAL STRUGGLES

Acknowledging the Complexity of Healing

The journey from healing to thriving is rarely straightforward. It is a path marked by ups and downs, breakthroughs, and relapses, particularly when navigating the intricate and often unspoken dynamics of psychological familial conflicts. Though unseen by others, these silent battles leave profound imprints on emotional, mental, and even physical well-being. Acknowledging the challenges is essential, but so is choosing to move forward with determination despite them.

Gratitude: A Cornerstone of Resilience

In such times, gratitude emerges as a cornerstone of resilience. It is not merely an act of thankfulness but a powerful spiritual and emotional practice—a divine reminder to thank Allah for the strength to heal, no matter how small the progress. Every step, however minor it may seem, is significant when viewed through the lens of gratitude energy.

The Transformative Power of Gratitude

When practiced consistently, gratitude becomes transformative. It illuminates the path forward, fostering a mindset of perseverance and hope. Healing is not an instantaneous process; it demands patience, steadfastness, and a commitment to growth. Patience does not mean waiting passively for healing to occur but actively working on personal goals while persevering through challenges. Together, steadfastness, patience, perseverance, and gratitude create a harmonious synergy that strengthens resilience and underscores the guiding presence of divine grace.

Celebrating Progress Throughout Struggles

Gratitude helps individuals recognize that even the most minor victories in healing and personal growth are monumental steps toward thriving. These small wins, often overlooked, are the building blocks of a resilient spirit. Consider the following examples:

> **Clarity in Chaos**: A brief moment of emotional clarity amidst turmoil is a sign of progress worth celebrating.

Healthy Boundaries: Setting even a single boundary within a toxic relationship is a profound achievement that fosters self-respect.

Self-Compassion: Offering oneself kindness and forgiveness in the face of self-doubt or criticism is a significant breakthrough in personal growth.

These small yet meaningful milestones form the foundation of a stronger, more resilient self. They are not merely markers of progress but evidence of inner strength and the capacity to thrive beyond the scars of past conflicts.

Gratitude as a Catalyst for Transformation

Gratitude goes beyond acknowledging progress; it redefines the narrative of healing. It reframes past struggles not as burdens to bear but as experiences that build strength and resilience. This shift in perspective reduces despair and fosters empowerment, transforming the healing process into a journey of self-discovery and hope. Gratitude is the catalyst that ignites this transformation, inspiring individuals to see their journey in a new light.

By embracing gratitude, setbacks become opportunities for learning and growth. Gratitude helps individuals see their journey as part of a greater purpose, encouraging forward momentum and inspiring faith in a brighter future. It is a tool that empowers individuals to turn setbacks into steppingstones, fostering a sense of resilience and strength.

Practical Steps to Cultivate Gratitude

Integrating gratitude into the healing process requires mindfulness and consistency. Here are some strategies:

Recognize Small Wins: Each day, note one joyous moment or accomplishment, no matter how minor it may seem.

Celebrate Progress, Not Perfection: Focus on growth and improvement rather than striving for unattainable flawlessness.

Practice Presence: Gratitude thrives in the present moment. Strengthen awareness of life's small blessings by embracing the here and now.

Connect to Faith: Gratitude is deeply rooted in faith. Regular prayer and reflection nurture a connection to divine guidance, comforting and reassuring during challenges.

Take Responsibility for Your Soul's Journey: Recognize that life is a test for the soul, and the responsibility lies in guiding it toward growth, resilience, and peace.

The Power of Gratitude in Healing

Gratitude is not about denying pain or overlooking struggles. Instead, it is about finding moments of grace and light throughout the darkness. Individuals draw strength from these moments by focusing on what has been gained rather than lost and building a foundation of hope and resilience.

Thriving Through Gratitude

Ultimately, gratitude is a compass guiding individuals toward inner peace, abundance, and fulfillment. Through gratitude, faith, and deliberate action, one can rise above the challenges of familial psychological conflicts to embrace a life filled with purpose, joy, and intention. Gratitude transforms survival into thriving, paving the way for a life of grace and resilience.

EMBRACE THE FUTURE WITH STRENGTH AND HOPE

The healing journey from covert bullying is a profound testament to resilience, courage, and transformation. By breaking free from the effects of manipulation, reclaiming autonomy, and establishing firm boundaries, survivors can rediscover their authentic selves and embrace a life of empowerment. Overcoming the lingering shadows of self-doubt, they unlock the potential to thrive personally and professionally, opening doors to a future filled with hope and optimism.

This transformative process marks the beginning of a new chapter, defined by genuine success that leads to personal fulfillment and financial achievement. With each step forward, survivors reaffirm their strength and prove that their best days lie ahead, filled with possibilities, prosperity, and the promise of a brighter, more inspiring future.

CREATING A FAMILY SANCTUARY

A family should be a sanctuary of trust, support, and emotional safety, but sometimes, covert bullying or emotional vampirism can fester within its dynamics. Emotional vampirism refers to behaviors where one person manipulates, drains, or sabotages others emotionally, often thriving on the pain or confusion they cause. This differs from emotional manipulation, a broader term that includes any attempt to control or influence another person's feelings or behaviors.

When emotional vampirism emerges within a family, especially in children who exhibit signs of this behavior, it can disrupt family dynamics, affecting the well-being of siblings and potentially leading to lasting emotional harm. However, with proactive attention and nurturing, families can prevent emotional vampirism from taking root and foster a healthy, balanced environment where every member feels valued.

Recognize the Signs Early

Children showing an inclination toward emotional vampirism often exhibit early signs, such as controlling behaviors, manipulative tendencies, or deriving satisfaction from others' discomfort. It is crucial to recognize these patterns early, empowering parents to take proactive steps before they grow into more significant, destructive dynamics:

Using manipulation to control others' emotions.
Sowing discord among siblings through subtle tactics.
Avoiding accountability and shifting blame.
Thriving on creating emotional confusion or distress.

It is vital to understand that children with these tendencies often do not realize the long-term harm they can cause. Early intervention can help redirect these behaviors into healthier emotional outlets.

Provide Emotional Guidance and Boundaries

Emotional vampirism thrives in a family setting where weak boundaries and a lack of accountability exist. Therefore, it's essential to provide clear boundaries that protect each member's emotional well-being:

Respect for boundaries is non-negotiable.
Emotions are discussed openly without manipulation or shame.

Family members are held accountable for their actions.
No one is allowed to use subtle control tactics or drain others emotionally.

When children with vampiristic tendencies are given clear emotional guidance and boundaries, it becomes easier to steer them toward healthier interactions. Encourage self-reflection, empathy, and an understanding of how their behavior affects others. Foster emotional intelligence by teaching them how to express needs without manipulation.

Protect the Emotional Balance Among Siblings

When emotional vampirism is present in one child, siblings often bear the emotional brunt, creating an imbalanced family dynamic. Siblings may become targets of manipulation, emotional outbursts, or undermining tactics, leaving them drained, confused, or resentful.

Encourage open dialogue between family members to prevent emotional undercurrents from festering.
Ensure no child is consistently in the shadow of another's emotional needs.
Help siblings identify unhealthy dynamics and give them tools to assert boundaries.
Foster mutual respect and emotional resilience so all children feel empowered.

By fostering a balanced environment, parents can prevent one child's manipulative behaviors from overpowering the rest of the family. Every child deserves to feel emotionally safe and supported in their home.

Empower Through Healthy Discipline, Not Hate

Preventing emotional vampirism from growing into a more significant issue requires discipline, but it must come from a place of love and understanding rather than hate or resentment. Children with these tendencies need guidance to learn healthier ways of interacting, not punishment that reinforces feelings of alienation.

Address behaviors without labeling the child as inherently evil or malicious.

Reinforce positive behaviors with praise and attention while addressing negative patterns firmly but lovingly.

Teach problem-solving, emotional regulation, and empathy as skills to develop, not as moral failings.

Empathy and emotional growth are essential here. A family can thrive if issues are addressed openly and constructively, preventing the child from wielding power through manipulation while still maintaining a foundation of love and acceptance.

Maintain a Healthy Family Environment

In addition to addressing emotional vampirism head-on, it is crucial to cultivate a broader, healthy family environment. This includes fostering emotional literacy, teaching compassion, and allowing everyone's feelings to be heard and respected.

Hold regular family meetings where everyone's voice is heard.

Encourage each family member to express their emotions openly and healthily.

Ensure that the family is a judgment-free zone where problems are solved together. Reinforce the value of collaboration, mutual support, and shared emotional responsibilities.

Be Mindful of Power Dynamics

Power dynamics can shift in families, and if left unchecked, emotional vampires can grow in influence, controlling or manipulating the household. Pay attention to power imbalances where one person consistently dominates emotionally through overt bullying or covert tactics.

Encourage equal participation in decision-making and family discussions.

Do not let one child monopolize attention or control the emotional tone of the household.

Ensure that parents lead by example, setting healthy boundaries and fostering mutual respect.

By maintaining balanced power dynamics and modeling healthy behavior, you prevent emotional vampires from gaining dominance.

Focus on Healing, Not Control

While emotional vampirism can be harmful, the goal is not to control or suppress the child displaying these tendencies but to guide them toward healthier emotional engagement. Healing comes from understanding, patience, and active efforts to foster emotional intelligence.

Focus on redirecting negative tendencies toward more positive outlets. Help them understand how their behavior affects others and empower them to build stronger, more fulfilling relationships within the family. This, in turn, can create a sanctuary where every family member feels safe, valued, and respected.

Conclusion: Building a Resilient and Compassionate Family

Preventing covert bullying and emotional vampirism in families is about awareness, proactive parenting, and fostering an emotionally safe environment. Families can avoid power imbalances and promote a positive atmosphere by addressing emotional manipulation early, protecting siblings, and guiding all children toward healthier interactions. Through clear boundaries, emotional intelligence, and mutual respect, even those prone to emotional vampirism can learn healthier ways of engaging with others. The goal is not to create resentment but to foster understanding, ensuring the family remains a sanctuary for everyone.

GLOSSARY

Covert Bullying: Indirect bullying through gossip, exclusion, rumors, and manipulation, targeting the target's self-esteem and emotional well-being.

Gaslighting: A psychological that causes someone to doubt their reality, using denial and false information to confuse and control them.

Target: An individual singled out for mistreatment due to perceived vulnerabilities or differences

Faminemy: A is a family member who appears supportive but secretly undermines and sabotages others within the family, acting as a covert adversary.

Frenemy: A frenemy is someone who pretends to be a friend but secretly harbors jealousy or rivalry, subtly undermining or manipulating while maintaining a facade of support.

REFERENCES

Scientific Explanations of Myths and Phenomena

Klein, B. Scientific Explanations of Supernatural Phenomena: Porphyria, Rabies, and Blood Disorders. Global Health Press, 2017.

Roberts, A. The Role of Porphyria and Anemia in Shaping Vampire Myths Throughout History. Medical Science Publications, 2012.

Sims, K. Rabies and Folklore: How Epidemics Shaped Vampire Myths and Other Supernatural Creatures. Journal of Folk Medicine, 2019.

Murray, J. Decay and Folklore: Natural Processes and the Vampire Myth. Historical Science Review Journal, 2015.

Family Dynamics and Psychological Impacts

Klein, B. Scientific Explanations of Jealousy and Competition in Family Relationships. Global Health Press, 2018.

Roberts, A. The Psychological Effects of Parental Jealousy on Children. Psychological Science Publications, 2016.

Sims, K. The Role of Parental Jealousy in Creating Psychological Tensions Within Families. Journal of Social Psychology, 2019.Murray, J. The Effects of Emotional Bullying Within Families: Analyzing Competitive and Jealous Behaviors Between

Parents and Their Children. Psychological Science Review, 2015.

Religious and Spiritual Teaching

Islam: Quran 13:11: "God does not change the condition of a people until they change what is in themselves."

Quran 94:6: "Indeed, with hardship comes ease."

Concept of Tazkiyah (purification of the soul).

Christianity: • Romans 12:2: "Do not conform to the pattern of this world, but be transformed by the renewing of your mind."

Hebrews 12:11: "No discipline seems pleasant at the time, but painful. Later on, however, it produces a harvest of righteousness and peace."

Judaism: Pirkei Avot 2:5: "Do not say, 'When I free myself, I will study,' for perhaps you will never free yourself."

Hinduism: Bhagavad Gita 6:35: "The mind is restless and hard to control, but it can be tamed through practice and detachment."

Buddhism: Dhammapada 1:1: "What you think, you become. What you feel, you attract. What you imagine, you create."

Sufism: Rumi: "The soul that is free of ego is the soul that is closest to God."

Taoism: Tao Te Ching 44: "When I let go of what I am, I become what I might be."

Native American Spirituality: "The longest journey you will make in your life is from your head to your heart."

Self-Help and Spirituality

Angela Duckworth. *Grit: The Power of Passion and Persever-ance.* Scribner, 2016.

Carol S. Dweck. *Mindset: The New Psychology of Success.* Random House, 2006.

Swami Satyananda Saraswati. *The Four Chapters on Free-dom: Commentary on the Yoga Sutras of Patanjali.* Bihar School of Yoga, 2001.

Joseph Murphy. "Your subconscious mind is your servant. Whatever you plant in it will grow."

Scientific and Psychological Research

Giftedness and Perfectionism:

Parker, W. D., & Mills, C. J. The incidence of perfectionism in gifted students. Gifted Child Quarterly, 40(4), 194–199, 1996. • Flett, G. L., Hewitt, P. L., & Martin, T. R. Perfectionism and maladjustment. Journal of Social Behavior and Personality, 1995.

Procrastination : Ferrari, J. R., & Díaz-Morales, J. F. Avoid-ance procrastination in adults. Behavioral Psychology, 2014.

Childhood Bullying and Mental Health:

Takizawa, R., Maughan, B., & Arseneault, L. The long-term ef-fects of childhood bullying on adult mental health. American Journal of Psychiatry, 2014.

Hazan, C., & Shaver, P. R. (1987). Romantic love conceptual-ized as an attachment process. Journal of Personality and So-cial Psychology, 52(3), 511–524.

Rigby, K. (2003). Consequences of bullying in schools. Canadian Journal of Psychiatry, 48(9), 583–590.

Fraley, R. C., & Shaver, P. R. (2000). Adult romantic attachment: Theoretical developments, emerging controversies, and unanswered questions. Review of General Psychology, 4(2), 132–154.

BMC Psychology. (2023). Attachment and need to belong as moderators of the relationship between thwarted belongingness and suicidal ideation. BMC Psychology, 11, Article 1080.

Learned Helplessness: Seligman, M. E. P. Learned helplessness. Annual Review of Medicine, 1972.

Mindfulness and Behavioral Change:

Daniel Siegel. *The Science of Mindfulness.*

James Clear. *Atomic Habits: An Easy & Proven Way to Build Good Habits & Break Bad Ones.*

• *Psychology of Religion and Spirituality* journal (various studies on the role of spirituality in mental health).

CLOSING THOUGHTS

Understanding past wounds is not just a step towards healing but a powerful tool for becoming the best version of oneself. It's an empowering journey that begins with acknowledging and consciously addressing emotional pain, but the deeper awareness of our mortality as human beings fuels our growth. Accepting the limited nature of our lives can bring about a radical shift in perspective, empowering us to focus on realizing our potential rather than becoming consumed by past tragedies or holding onto experiences that no longer serve us.

Life often confronts us with harsh challenges, both overt and covert, which leave deep imprints on our mental and spiritual health. While these challenges sometimes seem incomprehensible, they may, from a spiritual perspective, be viewed as lessons intended to refine and strengthen the soul. This perspective can provide a comforting and hopeful outlook to those who endure them, offering a light in the darkness of struggle.

Bullying, whether within the family or between communities and nations, is a hidden force that leaves a profound impact on the lives of its targets. Emotional energy vampires, often found in toxic relationships, exploit psychological and emotional boundaries to drain others' energy, preventing their progress or success while boosting their sense of control and power. This form of exploitation occurs on multiple levels, whether within the family unit or in relationships between communities and nations. Covert bullying is used as a tool for manipulation, keeping individuals, groups, or even nations in a constant state of vulnerability and weakness.

Accepting our existence's ambiguity and reconciling with the unknown grants us great inner strength. When we approach life's challenges with a reflective spirit, they can be seen as opportunities for growth rather than mere hardships. For instance, a job loss can be viewed as a chance to explore new career paths. This perspective helps us overcome pain and regain control over our lives. Recognizing life's inherent mystery opens the door to inner peace and enhances our ability to face the future with greater optimism and confidence in our potential.

Ultimately, true victory lies not in understanding everything but in the courage to face the unknown, transcend pain and choose growth despite obstacles. Life is not merely a series of events that happen to us but a canvas of continuous opportunity to become stronger, wiser, and more adaptable. This understanding liberates us from the constraints and pain of the past, making our lives a testament to our strength, resilience, and ongoing desire to grow.

Amy Law

ABOUT THE AUTHOR

Amy Law is a passionate writer and author focused on personal transformation and empowerment, particularly overcoming toxic influences hindering growth and development. Drawing from her own experiences, she offers profound insight into the emotional and psychological impacts of covert bullying, manipulation, and the destructive forces that drain individuals' energy and potential. Her work specializes in family dynamics and their deep influence on self-confidence, aspirations, and the ability to achieve success.

Amy's expertise shines in her ability to transform challenging experiences into inspiring lessons and practical tools that help others regain their balance and uncover their true potential. Her writing seamlessly combines a deep understanding of human psychology with actionable strategies that can be applied to everyday life. This unique blend resonates strongly with readers who have faced similar challenges.

Her rare talent for conveying ideas heartfeltly creates a sense of connection and understanding for her audience, motivating them to confront their fears and embark on their journey toward healing and liberation. In this book, Amy sheds light on the complex dynamics of energy vampires—those who subtly drain others' confidence, energy, and ambitions, especially within families where these relationships are often masked as acts of love.

Amy provides an innovative roadmap for breaking free from toxic relationships, guiding readers toward reclaiming their emotional and psychological independence. The book focuses on achieving balance between the mind and soul, emphasizing inner harmony as a critical element for personal and financial success. This reflects her holistic approach to life and well-being.

Amy Lou's insights stem from her exceptional ability to connect emotionally with readers profoundly. She highlights the power of self-awareness and the importance of setting healthy boundaries. She firmly believes that having the courage to sever ties with toxic influences—especially from family members—is a crucial step toward true freedom.

Through her writing style, Amy supports individuals seeking to rebuild their self-esteem, overcome limiting beliefs, and achieve abundance in all areas of life. As a gifted storyteller, she blends practical advice with spiritual and psychological wisdom, helping readers recognize the hidden forces holding them back.

www.ingramcontent.com/pod-product-compliance
Lightning Source LLC
Chambersburg PA
CBHW050441150626
46551CB00028B/790